I choose and read books on the basis of the integrity and credibility of the author as much as content. I have been a privileged friend and spiritual father of Randy Clark for many years. This man is a leader among us who walks in wisdom and power at a level that is rare in the history of Christianity. He has brought the subject and practice of total healing into wide acceptance amid the evangelical world as well as the medical community. His books and conferences have been the means of spreading the message of the Gospel of the Kingdom across the world.

The humble demeanor, the sincerity of presentation and the clear articulation of the complete Gospel mark Randy Clark as one whose works will remain to the edge of history and beyond. His life is as consistent as his message. May his life and ministry continue long and large on the landscape of the world and may his voice remain clear and incisive as he divides the Word of God with precision and clarity in preaching and writing. This book on a controversial subject is vintage Randy Clark and will cut a wide swath in the world of practical theology and provide answers to seeking saints all over this world.

Thanks, Randy, for another masterpiece and for remaining a voice worth hearing and giving us words worth reading!

JACK TAYLOR, PRESIDENT
Dimensions Ministries
Melbourne, Florida

As a classical Pentecostal, I have longed to see a definitive work on the baptism of the Holy Spirit. For years, the dialogue between Evangelicals and Cessationists has produced "more heat than light." Dr. Randy Clark and Dr. Jon Ruthven have produced a seminal work that will strongly support Charismatics and Pentecostals for years to come. This is a scholarly work of significant value to both academia and the lay reader. Dr. Howard Ervin shared an insight in one of his books years ago: "A man with an experience is not at the mercy of a man with an argument." *Baptized in the Spirit: God's Presence Resting Upon You with Power* marries both the experience (history) and the argument (sound theology).

BISHOP JOSEPH L. GARLINGTON, SR.
Presiding Bishop
Reconciliation! An International Network
of Churches and Ministries

I was raised in a classical Pentecostal home, for which I am thankful beyond words. The ultimate atmosphere to be raised in is a home where the Holy Spirit is recognized and honored. Having said that, I recognize that I have become richer in my understanding of the Holy Spirit by cross-pollinating with those outside of my own stream. Randy Clark has become a primary voice for me with his insightful teaching out of his strong theological background and, more importantly for my walk, a model to follow. I don't know of anyone who illustrates life in the Holy Spirit better than Randy. He is a constant inspiration to me in my journey with God. I highly recommend this wonderful book, *Baptized in the Spirit: God's Presence Resting Upon You with Power.*

BILL JOHNSON
Bethel Church, Redding, CA
Author of *When Heaven Invades Earth* and *God is Good*

Randy Clark's book *Baptized in the Spirit: God's Presence Resting Upon You with Power* is a valuable resource for all of us who love both the Word and the Spirit. This work is thorough, inclusive, and biblically and theologically sound. The imparting and filling of the Holy Spirit are central for fulfilling the Great Commission in our day.

JOHN ARNOTT
Founding Pastor and President
Catch the Fire

St. Bernard of Clairvaux wrote, "This kind of song only the touch of the Holy Spirit teaches, and it is learned by experience alone….Let those who have not experienced it burn with desire, not so much to know as to experience it." Randy Clark's book *Baptized in the Spirit: God's Presence Resting Upon You with Power* stirs up such a burning desire for the touch of God. At the same time, this book makes a precious contribution to the Holy Spirit's work of unity by explaining the diverse views of baptism in the Spirit and showing how they are not contradictory but complementary.

DR. MARY HEALY
Professor of Sacred Scripture
Sacred Heart Major Seminary

Randy Clark is one of the most catalytic carriers of the Kingdom of God in our time. He continues to make history, pioneering a passion for healing and Holy Spirit intimacy that has changed whole movements within the Church. With Randy there is always a "more Lord" dimension to be realized as he presses into a deeper knowledge and expression of the heart of God. His newest book, *Baptized in the Spirit: God's Presence Resting Upon You with Power*, is the fruit of decades of study and application, bringing clarity where there has been confusion. Along with Dr. Jon Ruthven, Randy makes it clear that the baptism of the Holy Spirit, and the resulting state of empowered participation in the divine nature, is at the heart of our salvation, of missions, and of the future work of God on the earth. Mastering a great diversity of opinion, Randy brings together powerful application that is accessible to all believers. This is theology made fun! Dive in, read, and pray, and expect to experience clarity, power, and joy.

CHARLES STOCK
Senior Team Leader
Life Center, Harrisburg, PA

For the present generation, the Holy Spirit has lit up the whole world, starting the fourth great awakening, using Dr. Randy Clark.

Reading *Baptized in the Spirit: God's Presence Resting Upon You with Power* awakens my thirst for more of the Holy Spirit. Randy Clark and Jon Ruthven illustrate how the Holy Spirit has set ordinary people on fire and transformed the course of history through them. Coauthored by one of the most influential revivalists in world history and a respected theologian, this book is extraordinary, invaluable, and a must-read for all Christians and skeptics intrigued by the Holy Spirit.

DR. ANDREW S. PARK
Professor of Theology and Ethics
United Theological Seminary

Randy Clark is a sovereign vessel of God. God used him in Toronto, and many Christians throughout the world were never to be the same again. God used him at Westminster Chapel, and many of us were never the same again. God used him in South America, and many Brazilians in particular have never been the same again. God will use Randy in this book, and if you read what he has to say and apply it, you will never be the same again.

DR. R. T. KENDALL
Minister
Westminster Chapel (1977–2002)

In this great gift to the Church, Dr. Randy Clark offers historical, theological, and practical teaching on the baptism of the Holy Spirit. This is not a book just for one denomination or group within the Body of Christ. It is a book for all Christians who want to have a deeper relationship with Jesus and a release of all the gifts that God wishes to work within them. Thank you, Dr. Clark, for blessing the Church with your wisdom and insights!

DR. DAVID F. WATSON
Academic Dean and Vice President for Academic Affairs
United Theological Seminary

With great expectation and gratitude to God we receive this book from Randy Clark. Few people in the world today can speak to us with such authority about the work of the Holy Spirit and the power that is unleashed in the lives of believers as can Randy. His ministry in all parts of the world has been a concrete, visible, and renewing manifestation of what he shares in these pages. I had the privilege of sharing with Randy the ministry in different parts of the world and seeing how the power of the Spirit manifested through his ministry in a fresh, healthy way, without any human manipulation and with extraordinary changes in people's lives. God has used his ministry tremendously throughout the world, awakening the lives of thousands upon thousands of believers and introducing them to a new dimension—that of the supernatural—in everyday life. Not only is Randy someone capable of sharing and imparting powerful spiritual experiences, but he also has the unusual ability to combine this gift with a deep knowledge of the Word of God that gives his praxis a solid theological foundation, seriousness, and a healthy perspective. Therefore, I want to strongly recommend the reading of this material, as well as its use to perfect the lives of believers for an effective ministry today.

Dr. Carlos Mraida
Pastor of the Church of the Centre of Buenos Aires, Argentina
Member of the Coordinating Board of
"Argentina We Pray For You"
Former Professor, Baptist International Theological
Seminary, Buenos Aires, Argentina

DESTINY IMAGE BOOKS BY RANDY CLARK

Power to Heal

The Essential Guide to the Power of the Holy Spirit (with Bill Johnson)

God Can Use Little Ole Me

Power/Holiness/Evangelism

Authority to Heal

BAPTIZED IN THE
SPIRIT

GOD'S PRESENCE
RESTING UPON YOU WITH
POWER

RANDY CLARK

DESTINY IMAGE® PUBLISHERS, INC.

P.O. Box 310, Shippensburg, PA 17257-0310

"Promoting Inspired Lives."

This book and all other Destiny Image and Destiny Image Fiction books are available at Christian bookstores and distributors worldwide.

Cover design by Eileen Rockwell
Interior design by Terry Clifton

For more information on foreign distributors, call 717-532-3040.

Reach us on the Internet: www.destinyimage.com.

ISBN 13 TP: 978-0-7684-1234-5
ISBN 13 eBook: 978-0-7684-1235-2
ISBN 13 HC: 978-0-7684-1524-7
ISBN 13 LP: 978-0-7684-1525-4

For Worldwide Distribution, Printed in the U.S.A.

2 3 4 5 6 7 8 / 21 20 19 18 17

CONTENTS

FOREWORD

by Dr. Craig Keener

Associate Professor of New Testament,
Asbury Theological Seminary

When John the Baptist announced that the One coming after him would baptize in the Holy Spirit, he probably understood that the One whose way he was preparing was God Himself (as in Isaiah 40:3). No one but God could pour out God's Spirit on His people (see Isa. 32:15; 44:3; Ezek. 39:29; Joel 2:28-29)!

John was not thinking in terms of only this or that aspect of the Spirit's ministry, of one experience or another. He was thinking of God's promise to fully empower His people with His own presence at the time of the end, the time when He would restore His people. This is why different New Testament passages may employ the language of "baptized in the Spirit," "receiving the Spirit," and so forth, in somewhat different ways. All of these ways are encompassed in the original promise. Our various traditions may draw on the language or emphasis of one passage or another, right in what we see but neglecting what others rightly see in different passages.

When we get past the nomenclature, though, most Christians agree: we receive the Spirit in some way at conversion, and we can also have subsequent experiences with the Spirit. We all desperately need God's power to fulfill God's work. Discussions about nomenclature have their place, but ultimately we don't need to focus on word definitions (cf. 1 Tim. 6:4; 2 Tim. 2:14) nearly so much as we need to embrace all that God has for us, whatever we call this experience of empowerment. Indeed, it should be clear from Acts that the Lord can baptize people on multiple occasions and with a variety of signs that indicate the Spirit's filling of people (see Acts 2:4; 4:8,31; 9:17; 13:9). In contrast to most traditional debates, even among scholars, Randy Clark strives to represent the range of views fairly. Instead of polemically reacting against various positions, he seeks to learn from whatever truth may be found in each of them.

After surveying views about the baptism in the Holy Spirit, however, Randy turns to praxis. He goes beyond the academic debates and whets our appetite for more of the Spirit by welcoming many Christians he knows to share their own encounters with the Holy Spirit. That each experience is different invites us not to imitate one experience but to seek our own encounter with the living God.

Although most Christians will appreciate testimonies of power for ministry, some readers may struggle with accounts of people being overwhelmed emotionally and even physically during some of these experiences. But think about it: Why shouldn't the power of the Third Person of the Trinity sometimes overwhelm us, affecting our whole person? Someday we will have bodies of glory able to withstand the fullness of God's glory, but our present nervous systems are just not wired for the full intensity of encounters with the infinite God. Many divine or angelic encounters even traumatize those who experience them (see Gen. 15:12; Ezek. 1:28; Dan. 8:16-18,27; 10:9).

When God showed up in a special way, the priests could not stand to minister in the temple (see 1 Kings 8:11; 2 Chron. 5:14).

When ungodly people came to the place where Samuel was leading younger prophets in sensitivity to the Lord, the Spirit's presence was so strong that even the ungodly fell down and began prophesying (see 1 Sam. 19:20-24). Some, like Samuel or Elisha (see 2 Kings 4:38), or even the Levite musicians in the temple (see 1 Chron. 25:1-6), had special gifts or roles in leading people into deeper intimacy with God's Spirit. God also often moved the prophets to various sorts of symbolic actions that we would consider quite strange if they weren't in the Bible (see 2 Kings 13:15-19; Jer. 13:1-11; 32:6-15; 35:1-19; Ezek. 6:3; 36:1,4; Acts 21:11). Not surprisingly, their contemporaries often thought the same thing (see 2 Kings 9:11; Jer. 29:26; Hos. 9:7; John 10:20; Acts 26:24).

No one is saying that we should spend our entire *life* lying on the floor, overwhelmed by God's glory, but there is certainly biblical precedent for experiencing God in an extraordinary way. Luke does not narrate all the behavior on the Day of Pentecost, as when Jesus's followers praised God in other languages, but it's no surprise that some people thought them drunk (see Acts 2:13). Being filled with the Spirit in worshipful ways offers a positive contrast to drunkenness (see Eph. 5:18-20).

For at least the past few centuries, many have experienced dramatic emotional and physical releases during revival movements, including at various times pretty much the range of experiences reported today. This has happened among Methodists, Presbyterians, and Baptists; in India, Indonesia, and the United States; and before, during, and, to an even greater extent, beyond the 20th century.

Different revival movements have had different characteristics: revivals of repentance have included people weeping over their souls as they sought salvation; contrastingly, the people in revivals focused on empowerment for missions often have experienced great joy. Joy is repeatedly linked with celebratory praise in the Psalms; why should it surprise anyone if the second-listed fruit of the Spirit shows up at times when the Spirit is poured out (see Gal. 5:22)? Perhaps we have needed such a reminder here in the West, where joy and laughter are associated with parties and sports events more than with our worship services, which are sometimes solemn.

In the 1970s, two days after my conversion from atheism, I was filled with the Spirit and so overwhelmed with God's majesty that I felt I could not offer worthy praise unless He gave me the words Himself. The words came out in another language; I had never heard of this gift before. Yet this worship was also filled with a deep, cathartic laughter, reflecting a joy I had never before experienced. Perhaps no one called it "holy laughter" in the 1970s, but why should what we call it suddenly make joy from the Spirit a matter of controversy?

I have experienced recurring episodes of empowerment and renewal during which I am overwhelmed deeply by the Spirit, sometimes weeping and sometimes feeling great joy. Sometimes the experience of God's presence and power was so intense—though so wonderful—that I could not stand it, and I would just beg for God to take me all the way home to Heaven so it would never stop.

On one of those occasions I felt desperate for strength and boldness to face the ministry challenges ahead. I wanted to remain inconspicuous in order to guard my academic reputation and also to avoid distracting others. When Randy Clark laid hands on me, I was deeply touched by the Spirit, and for quite some time I wept and laughed simultaneously as God spoke His tender love and assurances to my heart. I was strengthened for the tests that did indeed lie in the months that followed.

Although Randy naturally shares many stories from his own life and ministry, his goal is not to get you to honor Randy Clark. Randy's heart is for you to desire God's presence. Why would anyone refuse the touch of the Holy Spirit, who reaches to the very core of our being? God promises us that the Spirit is available to us if we ask Him (see Luke 11:13).

INTRODUCTION

Many of you who have picked up this book are experiential learners. You learn best in "hands-on" situations, in the midst of real life. That is why testimony is so powerful. So, before we tackle the issues of biblical interpretation and doctrinal positions regarding being filled or baptized in the Holy Spirit, I would like to share two experiences—two God encounters—from my wife DeAnne. The first was in 1988, the second in 1994.

In 1988, DeAnne and I moved to St. Louis to start a new church. It was to be the first Vineyard church in the greater St. Louis area and the second Vineyard in Missouri. We were only 33 and 31 years old at the time. We had worked hard during the two years prior to the move to "till the soil" for this new church. We did not know anyone in the St. Louis area at the time of our move. We had no team going with us, no worship leader, no support.

Prior to the move to St. Louis, during the eleven months of an over-300-mile round-trip every weekend, we had managed to gather about 11 people to be part of the new church. Two years later, with 40 people we felt led of Holy Spirit to reach out to unchurched people in a focused manner. We felt we wanted to increase in size in our new location, and so we developed a plan: DeAnne and I would undertake to call 20,000 people, with the help of about 12 others. We knew this would take us a few weeks at the very least. The hope was to find about 2,000 people out of the 20,000 who might be interested in visiting our new church. Out of this 2,000 we were expecting 90-100 people who would actually visit the church. We were set to have our first public service on Sunday morning in a month.

Part of the plan was for DeAnne to be the primary person to follow up with the 2,000 or so we hoped would indicate interest, and then, with the 90 or so people we hoped would actually visit the church. Even though we are positive thinkers, we were well aware of the daunting challenge that DeAnne was facing. She would need a special baptism of love for the people who responded, as well as divine enablement (grace) to accomplish the task before her.

The night before we were to begin calling, we met in a school with about 40 people. DeAnne was part of the small worship team. During worship, she suddenly began to weep. Then she collapsed to the floor and began not just to cry, but to wail. It was a loud wailing, accompanied by holy tears. It was so disruptive that the worship came to a stop. One of my leaders came to me and asked, "Do you want me to take her out of the room? Do you want us to carry her out to a private place?" I think there was some concern on his part that this might be a deliverance issue, or that there was a need for inner healing, due to the emotional wailing. I responded, "No, this is God, and I want the church to see how powerfully God can touch someone. People need to see the power of God." I then instructed everyone to point their hands toward DeAnne and gently pray, blessing what God was doing to her.

This particular filling or baptism in the Spirit that DeAnne experienced empowered her with a special love and grace to follow up with hundreds of phone calls to new parishoners over the next few weeks. What was impossible in the natural was accomplished in the spiritual as a result of a touch of God's Spirit.

Then, in 1994, DeAnne had a second powerful experience that occurred while I was traveling in Europe. Although this second experience was a potent encounter with God, it would be misrepresentative to say she had another baptism in the Spirit; it was more of a visitation of the Spirit that included holy tears, jubilation, and peace, and it lasted for days. When she called to tell me what was happening to her, I encouraged her to give herself to God and not worry about the church or the children because they would all manage. I knew as I listened to her that she was having a Holy Spirit visitation similar to what John Wimber's wife, Carol, had experienced. DeAnne's experience lasted for many days. I will let her tell you in her own words what happened:

> In August 2000, I had an encounter with God that forever changed my life. I had reached a point where I was overwhelmed by my sinful nature. I was broken and humbled before God. For three weeks I could not carry on with my responsibilities as a mother of four children and as co-pastor of the church that Randy and I had planted. I retreated to my room for three weeks, with worship music playing 24/7 and Bible and notepad in hand. For days I found myself weeping, reading the Word of God, and just sitting still before Him. Gradually, God began impressing Scriptures on me such as Song of Songs 5:2-6, Jeremiah 29:13, and Jeremiah 33:3. Then, He began to emphasize the story of Mary and Martha, especially Jesus' response to Martha's criticism of Mary (Luke 10:41-42 was magnified in my spirit). I began to realize that God was showing me that all my activities and all my earthly relationships would never fulfill me. My love for "doing" for Him had far outweighed my love for time alone with Him. The more time I spent alone in His presence, the more I realized

that if this was all I did for the rest of my life, I would be content. That was the lesson God had for me.

The following day, something lifted. I was able to return to my normal activities; however, one thing had changed: even though I was back doing the things a mom and a pastor needed to do, my one desire was to return quickly to that secret place, that alone time with God. I was no longer someone consumed with "doing" but was being transformed into someone content just to be with Him.

I believe this experience was given to prepare DeAnne for the move that was to come that would require us to resign from our church and move across the country to Pennsylvania. We received God's direction for this great change in our lives through prophetic revelation. It was to be a move that would profoundly impact DeAnne. She gave up her position as co-pastor of our church, which had grown to about 400 constituents. She was taken away from her place as a member of the preaching team and as one of the chief prophetic persons in the church. She also had to leave behind many close friendships. Essentially everything that had given her identity and purpose was left behind in St. Louis. God was gracious to prepare DeAnne for what was to come through His visitation that lasted weeks.

In the pages that follow, you will be privileged to hear many powerful testimonies of Holy Spirit baptism encounters, along with an examination of issues of biblical interpretation and doctrinial positions of baptism in the Holy Spirit. There is probably no other experience within the last 100 years of Christianity that has been more controversial than the subject of baptism in the Holy Spirit. Indeed, although incredibly important, this biblical concept has generated great confusion within the Church. It is my hope and prayer that by the end of our study together, the Holy Spirit will have enlivened your mind to God's great truths regarding the necessity of receiving all that He has for us and welcoming the blessings and empowerment that come with a touch from His Spirit.

Overcoming Doctrinal Differences

Christians have been divided over when the baptism in the Holy Spirit takes place, what the initial evidence of the baptism is, and what the process is that one goes through in receiving the experience of the baptism. I believe that the Western mindset, which seems to need to systematize its doctrine, is part of the cause of this division. We like our doctrinal expressions to be neat and tidy, logical and consistent. We want to box God into our own doctrinal interpretation of the Bible. Therein lies the root of the problem—God is greater than our doctrinal systems, regardless of whether that system is Roman Catholic, Orthodox, Evangelical, Reformed, Lutheran, Baptist, Methodist, Holiness, Pentecostal, or Restoration Movement.

Within these doctrinal systems we find a number of theological camps. On the one hand, the Orthodox, Catholics, Anglicans, Episcopalians, and Lutherans believe that one is baptized in the Holy Spirit at the time of infant baptism and that later there is a renewed filling, or a stirring up of the gift of the Holy Spirit, which one receives at confirmation. Dr. Mary Healy explains a variation of this view with regard to the Catholic Church as follows:

> The Catholic Church teaches that the Holy Spirit is given to a person at baptism, but it doesn't have a formal teaching about what "baptism in the Spirit" is or when it occurs. Some Catholic theologians would say it is identical with the sacrament of baptism; others would say it is identical with confirmation; others would say it is a subsequent experience that brings alive the gift of God received in baptism and confirmation; and still others would say that it differs from person to person.[1]

Evangelicals, Reformed, Baptists, and Modern Methodists form another group that believes one is baptized in the Holy Spirit at the time of conversion and that there can be many subsequent fillings of the Holy Spirit. A third group includes Holiness denominations such as Church of God (Anderson, Indiana), Nazarene, and others—most of which arise from the Wesleyan tradition, but also the Keswick movement that is Reformed in theology—which believe that when one is born again of the Spirit, at that time he or she is indwelt and sealed by the Spirit. However, there is a second definite work of grace of the Holy Spirit, usually called "sanctification," which perfects one in love, gives victory over the carnal nature, and empowers the Christian. (The Keswick movement would prefer language of *consecration* to *sanctification*.)

The fourth group, which includes Pentecostals, sees the baptism in the Holy Spirit as a clearly defined experience—one subsequent to conversion. They believe conversion is when one is born again, indwelt and sealed by the Holy Spirit. However, the baptism in the Holy Spirit must be sought as a distinct experience subsequent to conversion. According to this fourth group, the baptism in the Spirit is only rarely a simultaneous experience with conversion.

This fourth group of Pentecostals divides into two subgroups. The first subgroup has a Holiness background and sees three stages in the Christian experience: (1) conversion, (2) sanctification, and (3) the baptism in the Holy Spirit. The second subgroup, which has a more Baptist background, has a two-stage view: (1) conversion and (2) baptism in the Holy Spirit. In this latter view, sanctification is seen as progressive. The Assemblies of God and the Apostolic Church are in this second subgroup.[2]

A related question then emerges: "How does one know when one is 'baptized in the Holy Spirit'?" When we come to the subject of the "initial evidence" of the baptism in the Holy Spirit, the Pentecostals, most Protestant Charismatics, and some Roman Catholic Charismatics say that "speaking in tongues" is the initial evidence of the baptism. Evangelical Christian denominations tend to emphasize the fruit of the Spirit, especially faith, hope, and love, as the evidence of the baptism in the Holy Spirit. The third group, the Holiness group, emphasizes the evidence of the second definite work of grace as being perfected in love, giving power to always resist temptation and to better serve God and man.

While I was a student at The Southern Baptist Theological Seminary in Louisville, Kentucky, I met a graduate student, Larry Hart, who was working on his dissertation. His enthusiasm, love, joy, and Christian spirit really impressed me. We had several conversations while I was writing a term paper on the subject of the Charismatic movement. Larry was writing his dissertation on "A Critique of American Pentecostal Theology."

Larry, who is a Southern Baptist, shared with me that when he came to Southern Seminary, he argued for the baptism in the Holy Spirit as a subsequent experience to conversion, just as any Assembly of God minister would do. He had received his undergraduate degree in psychology from Oral Roberts University; he later became a chaplain there and served as an associate professor in the Theology Department at the university.

I was surprised when he stated he no longer believed the baptism in the Holy Spirit to be subsequent to conversion. Neither did he believe that tongues were the initial evidence of the baptism in the Holy Spirit, even though he did have the gift of tongues. I asked him what changed his mind, and he said, "The Bible." I asked what changed his mind about how he had been interpreting the Bible, and his answer was that he had read James Dunn's book *Baptism in the Holy Spirit*. He came to his conclusions because he had been unable to refute Dunn's exposition of Scripture. I believe Dunn's book is still one of the most important books on this subject. It is a meticulous exegesis of all the passages in the New Testament on this subject. It has also convinced me that the Pentecostal position demands that some Scriptures be given a meaning other than what appears to be the plain meaning of the context.

However, Howard Irwin's book *Conversion Initiation and the Baptism in the Holy Spirit,* which was written to refute Dunn's book, has also convinced me that the Evangelical position demands that some Scriptures be given a meaning other than what appears to be the plain meaning of the context. This has brought me to the realization that God is a God of diversity who does not have to fit His work into either the Pentecostal or the Evangelical position. He sometimes baptizes in the Holy Spirit at conversion and at other times baptizes in the Holy Spirit subsequent to conversion. Sometimes tongues accompany this baptism, and sometimes they do not. In my years of ministry I have encountered a great diversity in the ways in which people receive the baptism. Take, for instance, this testimony from Dr. Tom Jones's dissertation—not his personal experience, but that of one of the many persons he interviewed:

> The day I received the baptism in the Holy Spirit something broke. In fact, I have very little memory of things that happened in my childhood and things that happened before God touched me that day. It's truly like I was born again. And I think that what happened to me that night was, I believe—it was my salvation although I think there are those who would disagree. Most people call it my baptism of the Holy Spirit. I think I got both salvation and Holy Spirit baptism at the same time. I experienced true conversion and I was filled with the Holy Spirit at the same time. There was just a radical difference: holiness, passion, every time there was any event going on; I didn't care what church it was at, what they were preaching—I just wanted to hear, and I wanted to worship. Worship became everything. I didn't get my prayer language that night or start speaking in tongues, but as I began praying at home, very shortly after that I was baptized in the Holy Spirit with the evidence of speaking in tongues in my home, after that first touch.

So everything changed, and my heart was broken for the poor.[3]

It is interesting that this experience was so powerful that it caused the man to question whether or not he had really been saved, and from that point on he believed that the moment of baptism in the Spirit was the moment of his real conversion. One of my favorite missionaries, Deena Van't Hul, felt the same way. Her moment of Holy Spirit baptism changed her life and was so powerful that it caused her to question whether or not she was really saved prior to this event.[4]

When John Wesley was converted, at the church on Aldersgate Street, he considered it his sanctification, but he also considered it his real salvation. He described his experience as a feeling of his heart being "strangely warmed," and this introduced an emphasis on the Holy Spirit in Wesley's theology.[5]

Paulos Hanfere, one of my spiritual sons, had a very different experience than that of Wesley, and his experience included the reception of the prayer language.

> I received my prayer language when I was 12 years old. However, while growing up I never experienced the power of God in my life that was promised in Acts 2. I lived with little to no victory in my Christian walk and no real desire to pursue the things of God. It was not until after I finished college and went to work in the marketplace that things began to change. In 2005 I connected with Global Awakening by attending one of their VOA conferences. It was at this conference that God began to open me up to the fact that there is "more" of Him to be experienced in this Christian life. Thus began my pursuit of God. I started going from conference to conference, church to church, violently seeking the power of God (see Matt. 11:12). In October 2010, I attended

a Global Awakening conference where Dr. Clark was speaking. During the second night of the conference, in my hotel room, desperate for an encounter with God, I begin crying out for more, reading Scripture out loud until the early hours of the morning. On the last day of the conference, while Dr. Clark was ministering, he asked all those who were sensing or feeling the power of God on them to come to the front to be prayed for.

I had been through this impartation altar call many times before without feeling or sensing anything, and I thought it would be the same this time as well. There was a woman sitting in my row who was going up for prayer, and when I tried to stand to allow her to pass, to my surprise I couldn't stand. I tried again, and it felt like there were 300-pound weights tied to each of my legs. With the weightiness of the glory of God upon me, I continued to try with every ounce of strength in my body to reach the front. Finally, I made it. When Dr. Clark turned to me and moved his hand to bless the power of God that was on me, I shot back about four to five feet and began to shake violently on the ground and sweat profusely. I felt waves of high-power electrical currents flowing up and down my body from head to toe. My heels hit the ground so hard and fast that they were bruised and sore for weeks afterward. It didn't stop there; I would wake up out of my sleep shaking under the power of God. This occurred along with other manifestations.

Life was never the same again. I couldn't read Scripture without weeping, as it had come alive. I couldn't pray without weeping and felt such a sense of gratitude and awe toward God. I noticed that I was bolder when sharing and speaking about Jesus. Every time I would pray for people at church or out on the street they would cry because they sensed the love and presence of God. Finally, I walked in victory over sin that I had battled with for much of my life, experiencing freedom for the first time.[6]

Clearly, the Spirit was received by each of these individuals, deepening and enriching their relationship with God and giving them power over personal sin and empowerment for ministry. Yet the ways in which the Spirit touches a person and the timing of His touch(es) vary, I believe, according to God's sovereignty and our response to His divine initiatives.

Before we move on, let us take note that there is now a fifth group composed of a growing number of people who hail from non-Charismatic, conservative Evangelical backgrounds who have adopted certain Classical Pentecostal practices such as healing the sick, casting out demons, and receiving prophetic revelations. Many of these people believe that the so-called baptism in the Holy Spirit happens at conversion and is not the second work of grace subsequent to the new birth. They also believe that tongues are simply one of many spiritual gifts and not the only evidence of a particular spiritual experience. Many of these people still see themselves as conservative Evangelicals, theologically and culturally, and have sought to relate their experiences of the Holy Spirit's power to conservative Evangelical beliefs.[7]

My friend and colleague, theologian Dr. Jon Ruthven, proposes a major departure from these traditional theologies, advocating a move toward a doctrine of the baptism of the Spirit that is emphasized in the Bible, toward the use of the term as Jesus presented it. In this view, the baptism of the Spirit is not simply an optional add-on to salvation but the very goal of the Bible, the central experience of the New Covenant, and the ideal expression of a truly Christian disciple. In Part Three of this book, Jon gives an in-depth picture of how this theology clearly emerges from the emphasis of the Bible itself.

In the pages that follow, we will walk through different definitions of the baptism of the Holy Spirit and the different ways the baptism may be appropriated, with both historical examples and modern-day examples of baptism that illustrate how the Holy Spirit has been, and continues to be, instrumental in major moves of God. In Luke 24:49, Jesus says, *"And behold, I am sending forth the promise of My Father upon you; but you are to stay in the city until you are clothed with power from on high"* (NASB). The "promise of My Father" that Jesus referenced included a series of Old Testament promises (Isaiah 44:3, Jeremiah 31:33, Ezekiel 36:27, and Joel 2:28) that were fulfilled in Acts 1:4 and are ours today. We should gladly receive all that we have access to through Holy Spirit baptism, laying aside doctrinal hindrances and pressing into the fullness of the mighty power from on high that is ours through Christ Jesus. F. F. Bosworth says, "God is waiting to pour out the Holy Spirit in fullness upon us. He comes as Christ's executive to execute for us all the blessings provided by Calvary."[8]

PART ONE

BAPTIZED IN THE HOLY SPIRIT

Dr. Randy Clark

Chapter 1

The Evangelical, Holiness, Pentecostal, and Catholic Perspectives on the Baptism in the Holy Spirit

He who has been sanctified, his sins being put away
in baptism, and has been spiritually reformed into
a new man, has become fitted for receiving the Holy
Spirit; since the apostle says, "As many of you have
been baptized into Christ have put on Christ."[1]

—Cyprian

An Evangelical Perspective— Approximately 285 Million Adherents

My former professor at The Southern Baptist Theological Seminary, Dr. Lewis Drummond, gives the following definition of the baptism in the Holy Spirit—one that is a solid representation of the Evangelical position, especially that of the Southern Baptists:

This truth was first referred to by John the Baptist (Matt. 3:11). Then it was confirmed by our Lord

(Acts 1:4,5) with reference to the initial enduement of the Spirit at Pentecost. Basically, it is the receiving of the Spirit by the believer (Acts 2:38; 1 Corinthians 12:13). It is analogous to "being made to drink into the one Spirit." *It is thus experienced by all true believers. It is also the act and experience whereby the believer is united with Christ and incorporated into the Body of Christ* (1 Cor. 12:12; Gal. 3:27,28). Further, it involves reception of power, since the Spirit is the powerful presence of God in us (Acts 1:5,8). It occurs at conversion to all believers.[2]

According to R. A. Torrey, a famous evangelist in the late 1800s and early 1900s, the Bible is quite clear about the baptism. He states that the baptism is a definite experience, and you will know whether you have received it or not.[3] Torrey sees a difference between being born again by the Holy Spirit and being *baptized* in the Holy Spirit. Baptism in the Holy Spirit produces power (power over personal sin and empowerment for ministry) and is every believer's birthright.[4] Let's look at the testimony of Timothy Berry, one of my spiritual sons, for an illustration of Torrey's statements:

In November 2005, at the age of 19, I was driving my car down the interstate while worshiping the Lord. All of a sudden I began to cry. I had no idea why. Then, my body began to tingle all over, and I started to shake all over. It was an incredible feeling yet terrifying because I was driving fast and I didn't want to have an accident. I didn't know what I was experiencing. It was as if I didn't have control of my senses or my emotions or my body. As unusual as it was, I knew it was God because even though it was different and new, it felt good. I felt closer to God in that moment than since the day I had rededicated my life six years prior, at the age of 13. As I continued to weep, shake, and experience God's presence, I started to think about healing, although I had no idea why because I didn't believe in healing.

This experience lasted about 10 to 15 minutes. I finally had to pull my car over to an emergency lane, where I sat and wept like a baby. All I could think about was healing. Prior to this, I had been crying out to God for freedom from bondage in several areas of my life—things like pornography, desires of the flesh, and cares of the world. I was addicted to video games and sports and would play and watch them for hours a day. I was such an avid college football fan I would paint my whole body in my school colors just to watch a game. After my experience of the Holy Spirit in the car, I had no desire to play video games and no desire to watch sports or engage in any of the things that had bound me. I stopped going to football games and stopped playing video games. My friends thought I was in crisis with God. However, I had met God, and all I wanted was Him. My prayer life changed too. I started praying sometimes for two to three hours at a time. I was possessed with a hunger for Him like never before.

One of the biggest fruits of this experience that happened immediately was the way in which I read Scripture with a new lens. The Scriptures were life to me for the first time. In the past, I had so often walked away from reading the Bible because I felt condemned, ashamed, and guilty for my sin and the ways that my life did not reflect the life of Jesus. Prior to my experience in the car, I had been ashamed of my inability to overcome my flesh, but all that shame began to give way to God's truths.

Theologically I believe I was baptized/filled with the Holy Spirit in my car because the fruit was a deliverance or sanctification experience. I knew I was changed. I couldn't explain it at the time, but I knew something was different in me. About a month later, I began to speak in tongues, but there was not an internal or external feeling/emotion/presence like what I had felt in the car. This was theologically confusing to me because the Pentecostals I talked to said my first experience was not *the* baptism of the Holy Spirit because I had not spoken in tongues. For me, though, the fruit of my experience in the car was more fruitful than the gift of tongues. Over time I have fallen in love with the gift of tongues, and it has helped edify my spirit, helped me experience God's presence, and allowed me a greater intimacy with God, but my first baptism of the Holy Spirit was a sanctification experience without tongues.

In 2006, about six months after my baptism experience in the car, I met Randy Clark at a conference in South Carolina. When he prayed for me during a time of impartation, I experienced the same overcoming presence of God, with weeping. After the conference, I began to travel on mission trips with Global Awakening, and I experienced the power and presence of God as I ministered to people. Looking back now, I see the tremendous fruit from that initial baptism experience in the car. Hundreds of souls have been saved as I have ministered, hundreds have experienced deliverance and healing, and many have experienced the baptism in the Holy Spirit.

My heart was changed in the car that day. I was a different person when I got out than when I got in. I fell in love with God and have come to understand that He loves me in a whole new way. The greatest fruit of my experience with the Holy Spirit is not His gifts or His power: it is His love. I am a changed man because of the love of God expressed to me through the personal presence of the Holy Spirit. Daily I get to cry out, "Abba, Father."

I pray that my story will encourage others to come to know God as I do—to understand that we are children of God, who unconditionally loves us and accepts us. Be encouraged—the Holy Spirit is in you for you and upon you for others. I pray that all will experience the Holy Spirit for their own sake and also for empowerment for ministry, to see people saved, healed, and delivered.

One could ask if Timothy's experience of the baptism was an Evangelical experience or a Pentecostal experience, etc., but regardless of what "box" we want to put it in, however we try to categorize it, what is important to Timothy is that he received his birthright as a believer.

Let's look at three other prominent perspectives on the baptism.

A Holiness Perspective—Approximately 12 Million Adherents

The Holiness movement, which has produced over 65 denominations, has its primary root in 19th-century Methodism. However, during the 19th century, the Methodist denomination was undergoing a radical shift away from its Wesleyan roots with its emphasis upon a second definite work of grace. Also, the editor of the denomination's official magazine was liberal and was very negative about the teaching on healing that had entered the Holiness movement during the last quarter of the 19th century at the Holiness camp meetings.

The secondary root of the Holiness movement comes from a more Calvinist heritage—the Keswick movement, which originated in England, where yearly meetings were held for the purpose of promoting personal holiness. A. T. Pierson, an early writer on healing in the atonement and a friend of the Pentecostal movement that was to follow, wrote in 1903 that the movement probably had its true origin in the 1858 revival that swept the United States and Great Britain. The initial teachings of the American Methodist evangelist R. Pearsall Smith and his wife, Hannah Whitall Smith, were instrumental in setting the stage for the hunger for greater personal holiness. He dated the beginning of the movement from 1873.[5] The popular phrase associated with the Wesleyan and Calvinist roots of the Holiness movement was "the deepening of the spiritual life."

A Pentecostal Perspective—Approximately 500 Million Adherents

The great Azusa Street revival at the turn of the century marks the birth of the Pentecostal Church. The phenomenon of tongues accompanied by the personal Pentecost that occurred at Azusa would forever change the spiritual landscape of the Church, giving rise to Pentecostalism and eventually the Charismatic movement. Within Pentecostalism is found the Assemblies of God, considered the largest Pentecostal denomination in the world.[6] The following quotation is from the "Statement of Fundamental Truths" of the Assemblies of God, with which many Protestant and some Catholic Charismatics would agree:

> All believers are entitled to and should ardently expect and earnestly seek the promise of the Father, the baptism in the Holy Spirit and fire, according to the command of our Lord Jesus Christ. This was the normal experience of all in the early Christian church. With it comes the enduement of power for life and service, the bestowment of the gifts and their uses in the work of the ministry (Luke 24:49; Acts 1:4,8; 1 Corinthians 12:1-31). *This experience is distinct from and subsequent to the experience of the new birth* (Acts 8:12-17; 10:44-46; 11:14-16; 15:7-9). With the baptism in the Holy Spirit come such

experiences as an overflowing fullness of the Spirit (John 7:37-39; Acts 4:8), a deepened reverence for God (Acts 2:43, Heb. 12:28), an intensified consecration to God and dedication to His work (Acts 2:42), and a more active love for Christ, for His Word, and for the lost (Mark 16:20).[7]

It is of note that the Assemblies of God cautions against becoming enamored with charismatic manifestations, with First Corinthians 2:2 as their basis, while viewing fidelity to God's Word as the plumb line for determining both personal and corporate Holy Spirit revival that flows from the baptismal experience.[8]

In her doctoral thesis, Heidi Baker shares a similar quote, this one from Pastor David Barrett, which also captures the position Pentecostals take on the baptism:

> A Christian confession or ecclesiastical tradition holding the distinctive teaching that all Christians should seek a post-conversion religious experience called the "Baptism with the Holy Spirit," and that a Spirit-baptized believer may receive one or more of the supernatural gifts known in the early church; instantaneous sanctification, the ability to prophesy, practice divine healing, speak in tongues (glossolalia), or interpret tongues.[9]

Pentecostals generally see a distinction between rebirth and the baptism in the Spirit. They see the baptism as being filled like the apostles were on the Day of Pentecost. The baptism on the Day of Pentecost was once and for all, but "equally the appropriation of the Spirit by believers is always for all."[10] Pentecostals see that this experience is the gateway to the gifts of the Spirit; they believe each Christian should seek such a post-conversion experience.

Testimonies from the early days of Azusa provide examples of these "gateway" experiences. One such testimony involves Edward

Lee and Jennie Evans Moore, the woman who would become William Seymour's wife.

> On April 6, 1906, a man named Edward Lee spontaneously burst forth in an unknown tongue after Seymour prayed for him. That evening as Seymour testified, Lee spoke in tongues again and the believers were swept to their knees. Jennie fell to the floor and immediately began speaking in all six languages she had seen [in a vision]. Each message in tongues was interpreted in English. After this, Jennie, who had never played the piano before, went to the keyboard and played the instrument while singing in tongues.[11]

She was the first woman known to speak in tongues in Los Angeles, and her Holy Spirit baptism experience, along with Lee's experience, was a spark that helped ignite the fires of the Great Azusa Street revival that followed.

A Catholic Perspective—Approximately 1.2 Billion Adherents

For those in the Catholic Charismatic Renewal, "baptism in the Spirit has been received and understood as the central grace at the heart of the Renewal."[12] The baptism of the Holy Spirit has been "experienced as a sovereign gift of God, not dependent on any human merit or activity."[13] Therefore, it is available to the whole Church, not one specific camp.[14] Accepting the baptism is "embracing the fullness of Christian initiation, which belongs to the Church."[15]

Characteristics of the baptism include being overcome with calmness, confidence, peace, and joy.[16] When people are baptized in the Spirit, their lives become marked as they experience a greater union with God and discover the Spirit's charisms, some of which include prophecy, healing and other gifts, and praise and worship.[17] According to the book about the Catholic Charismatic Renewal *Baptism in the Holy Spirit*, the phrase "baptism in the Spirit" is adapted from the verbal phrase "baptize in the Holy Spirit." This phrase can be found six times in Scriptures.[18]

As Dr. Heidi Baker states in her doctoral thesis, "several noteworthy Catholic mystics spoke of an infilling or baptism of the Holy Spirit." Baker goes on to point out that "Julian of Norwich (1343–1413 and Margery Kempe (1373–1439) were both influential Catholic mystics who believed in an infilling of the Holy Spirit. Julian supported Kempe and confirmed that she had a gift of tears, which was given to her by God."[19] There has been a great deal of evidence in the past regarding the gift of tears, tears that express great emotion and love, feelings beyond words. As Yves Congrar explains, "In this respect, then, tears are clearly related to speaking or praying in tongues."[20]

Baker quotes Catholic theologian William O'Shea: "The difference between baptism and confirmation is the difference between giving life and enabling that life to reach its full potential. Confirmation gives us the power to be what we already are in baptism."[21]

The Roman Catholic scholar Yves Congar acknowledges that Pentecostals insist on the distinction between rebirth and the baptism in the Holy Spirit.[22] For Catholics, the rite of being baptized in the Spirit comes with great peace and joy. The baptism "has come forth in a simple and powerful way to renew the lives of millions of believers in almost all of the Christian churches."[23] The testimony of Francis MacNutt illustrates this beautifully. As a young Catholic priest, Francis, in pursuit of Christ's directive to "love our neighbors as ourselves" (see Mark 12:31; Matt. 22:39), met a woman named Jo Kimmel, a Protestant layperson who was involved in the ministry of healing the sick. Over the course of conversations with Kimmel, and after reading, at Kimmel's urging, John Sherrill's *They Speak with Other Tongues*, Francis decided to investigate this extraordinary experience for himself. Believing that theology is supposed to be a reflection of things that are really happening, he began to earnestly ask if the charistmatic gifts that these people were giving witness to were authentic. Eventually Francis felt he wanted the baptism himself.

I didn't have an opportunity to pray for the Baptism of the Spirit until the following summer. Jo Kimmel was going to take her mother-in-law to a retreat called "A Camp Farthest Out." Jo's mother-in-law fell sick, so Jo wrote and asked me if I would like to take the available spot at the camp being held in Tennessee. There were 800 participants at the event, very large in my experience. I soon found out that the reason why it was so large was because of the quality and reputation of the three speakers: Rev. Tommy Tyson, a Methodist minister; Agnes Sanford, a remarkable Episcopalian about seventy years old whose special gift was inner healing and teaching about it; and Derek Prince, who taught about deliverance (a new topic for me).... I was filled with joy when I heard these speakers, so much so that I actually hated to hear them stop! All of them soon became my friends.... I had determined when I went there that my goal was to pray for the baptism of the Holy Spirit because it is supposed to deepen your relationship with Jesus. I wanted that! If that was the purpose of the baptism, then I knew I wanted it, even though I could not sort out all of the theological questions I had.

At the beginning of this camp they passed a microphone around so that each person could tell the entire group what they had come to receive. When the microphone finally came to the back of the auditorium where I was sitting, I took it, stood up, and said, "I am a Roman Catholic priest, and I came to receive the baptism of the Holy Spirit, whatever that is." When I made my prayer request known, it seemed to me that all 800 people turned around to look at me; they were amazed to see a Catholic priest there saying that kind of thing.

A man down in front, who was one of the four counselors assigned to pray with people (an Episcopal priest about eighty years old), stood up. He said, "I am just delighted that we have a Roman Catholic brother here this afternoon, and if Brother Francis will allow me the honor of praying for the baptism of the Spirit, I would be so pleased." Father Bill Sherwood, this Episcopal priest, had his little appointment book out, and I made an appointment to meet with him the following Wednesday morning at eleven o'clock.

Wednesday came around and I went to my appointment accompanied by Jo Kimmel and my camp roommate, an impressive Episcopal minister, along with a small group of other recipients. Father Bill Sherwood began by offering an explanation of what the baptism of the Spirit was, and as I waited I thought, "When is he going to get around to do the praying?" Finally, about 20 minutes before noon, they finally got around to praying. We prayed as a group for about five minutes in total. This confused me, and I mention this because we often seem to box in the Spirit or expect Him to follow our schedule or method. Instead, the Holy Spirit takes us where we are, with our own needs and works; sometimes it happens according to our own human expectations, but sometimes there is a better or different way.

After his prayer, they all turned to me and said, "Can you pray in tongues?" I answered, "Well, I came here to do what I could to receive the Spirit," so they said, "Go ahead and pray," so I did. I prayed very fluently in something that sounded to me like Russian—I don't know what it was. At that time I didn't have any welling up inside me or any great interior experience. What I was after was not tongues so much as a real encounter with Christ. That's what I was really looking for, so I left that session feeling disappointed.

Next, I went to the cafeteria—there were two lines of about 400 people in each line waiting to be fed. As I was waiting, Agnes Sanford cut into the line next to me. As one of the three main speakers, she had the option of cutting in so she could go and rest after the meals. I told her about the prayer appointment I had just experienced, and she said, "Well, I had a feeling from the first time I met you, at the beginning of this camp, that probably you should not have gone into a group and received prayer for the baptism of the Spirit the way they usually pray; that is, as if you don't already have the Spirit. I didn't want to stop you because I felt you were being moved in that direction, but now that you have brought it up, I feel that my initial leading was right when I felt the right prayer would be for you to receive the release of the gifts of the Holy Spirit that were already in you, by virtue of your baptism and ordination. Somehow these gifts need to be released fully. This prayer assumes that you do have the Spirit but that the gifts need to be released."

The next evening Mrs. Sanford and two people prayed for me. Agnes prayed a beautiful prayer for the unfolding of the gifts that were already within me, and in that prayer there were some elements of prophecy. The main one was that I would be used to bring the gift of healing back to the Catholic Church (a prophecy that has largely taken place)!

When she finished her prayer, a spirit of joy fell on all four of us in that room—we just laughed and laughed.

Then we would share for a while and we would begin to laugh again. A sense of well-being and joy filled me. This was the way the Spirit came to me—a sense of absolute joy. We decided that what had happened was that the Holy Spirit already in me was now fully released! Since that time my life has not been the same—particularly my ministry. It is hard to decide what causes what, but that isn't too important as long as the Spirit really becomes active!...I see a tremendous hope for the renewal of a real spiritual ministry where we can know Jesus Christ in a more personal way than we have ever known Him before, which isn't to say that we haven't known Him at all, but it is to say there is much more![24]

What are we to take away from these various definitions and experiences of the baptism of the Holy Spirit? I believe that taken together, all of these definitions reflect God's desire (which He has placed in our hearts) for us to effectively steward His supernatural gifts to the glory of His name. We may not agree on place, evidence, or process, but we do agree that we desire to welcome the precious Holy Spirit and His empowerment for life and ministry. Second Timothy 1:6 reminds us that God's gifts given to us are not kept or exercised by our own strength, but only by the power of the Holy Spirit dwelling within us.

Thomas Kidd, professor of history at Baylor University, has this to say about the issue of Holy Spirit baptism: "it is tough to have a vibrant theology of walking in the Spirit if much of your teaching on the Spirit focuses on what others should not be doing."[25] Let us strive to move beyond our differences and together embrace all that the precious Holy Spirit makes available to us in Jesus, and in so doing, allow the Spirit to facilitate the hand of God as together they mold and shape us into the vibrant Bride of Christ.

Chapter 2

THE TRADITIONAL AND RECENT PENTECOSTAL PERSPECTIVES OF THE BAPTISM IN THE HOLY SPIRIT

William W. Menzies, a Pentecostal scholar, believes the baptism of believers in the Holy Ghost (in the Upper Room, on the Day of Pentecost) is witnessed by the initial physical sign of speaking with other tongues as the Spirit of God gives them utterance (see Acts 2:42). The speaking in tongues in this instance is the same, in essence, as the gift of tongues but different in purpose and use (see 1 Cor. 12:4-10,28).[1]

Some Protestant Charismatics and most Roman Catholic Charismatics would not regard tongues as the *initial necessary* evidence but rather *an* evidence of the baptism of the Holy Spirit. This group believes that the baptism may occur simultaneously with conversion or subsequent to conversion, depending on the individual's expectancy and other criteria. I personally believe it is possible to experience the phenomenon of tongues without being baptized in the Holy Spirit.

An important leader in the Roman Catholic Church, Cardinal Léon-Joseph Suenens, teaches that the baptism in the Holy Spirit occurs at water baptism and is renewed at confirmation. (According to Catholic theology, the experience of regeneration/conversion occurs at infant baptism.) Cardinal Suenens writes in his book *A New Pentecost?*:

> Thus what many Catholics need to do is to realize that, for us, as well as the majority of Christian Churches, there is not a duality of baptisms, one in water and one in the Spirit. We believe there is but one baptism. Baptism in the Holy Spirit is not a sort of superbaptism, or a supplement to sacramental baptism which would then become the pivot of the Christian life.... Our one and only baptism is at the same time both paschal and Pentecostal. To avoid from now on all ambiguity, it would be better not to speak of "baptism in the Holy Spirit" but to look for another expression....Different expressions are being used to define this experience of baptism in the Spirit: the grace of actualizing gifts already received, a release of the Spirit, a manifestation of baptism, a coming to life of the gift of the Spirit received at confirmation, profound receptivity or docility to the Holy Spirit.[2]

The Old Testament makes mention of places in Scripture that the Spirit is discussed. Isaiah 44:3 states, *"For I will pour water on him who is thirsty, and floods on the dry ground; I will pour My Spirit on your descendants, and My blessing on your offspring"* (NKJV). Joel 2:28-29 also states, *"I will pour out My Spirit."* A common theme in these texts is "that the outpouring of the Spirit will bring a new knowledge of God."[3]

In the New Testament, the Gospel of John indicates that to "baptize with the Holy Spirit is to immerse into the very life of God."[4] Further, "Jesus explains to Nicodemus that the gift of the Spirit is linked with water baptism, which brings about a spiritual rebirth (John 3:5)."[5] The New Testament also discusses baptism in Luke when it mentions three things that the apostles needed to be instruments of the living Christ. One of these was to be baptized with the Holy Spirit, the second was verification that Jesus was really alive and triumphant over death, and the third was more instruction about the Kingdom of God.[6] Regarding the baptism in the Holy Spirit, Luke 3:16 states: *"I baptize you with water; but One is coming who is mightier than I, and I am not fit to untie the thong of his sandals; He will baptize you with the Holy Spirit and fire"* (NASB). Then in Acts Luke says, *"They saw what seemed to be tongues of fire that separated and came to rest on each of them"* (Acts 2:3).

Testimonies out of the great Azusa Street revival gave witness to times when "flames of fire would actually shoot out of and in through the roof of the warehouse" where the meetings were held and many were getting touched by God.[7] This was not natural fire but supernatural fire of the same kind Moses encountered with the burning bush—the bush that was burning but that was not consumed. These types of "fire sightings" are not unheard of. People in St. Louis called the fire department when they saw fire on the roof of the first and the largest Charismatic church in the area. The pastor of the largest Baptist church in South Africa saw fire on the top of his church during a meeting we were conducting. Neither of these buildings experienced actual burning that damaged the structure. This was holy fire that did no physical damage to the buildings.[8]

According to the Evangelical John Piper, "being baptized with the Holy Spirit is when a person, who is already a believer, receives an extraordinary spiritual power for Christ-exalting ministry."[9] Piper believes this to be true because being filled with the Spirit can bring "extraordinary power in ministry."[10]

Frank Macchia, an Assemblies of God theologian, believes that divine love is the gift of the Spirit. In his work *Baptized in the Spirit: A Global Pentecostal Theology*, he suggests, "Our final conclusion will be that Spirit baptism is a baptism into the love of God that sanctifies, renews, and empowers until Spirit baptism turns all of creation into the final dwelling place of God."[11]

With this belief comes the idea that Macchia presented, which is that glossolalia is a "symbol of empowered ministry that bridges linguistic and cultural boundaries."[12] He further explains that tongues were characteristic in the New Testament and can be for us now; however, "tongues cannot be turned into a law that governs how Spirit baptism must be received without exception within the actions of a sovereign God."[13]

I agree with Macchia in that the gift of tongues is not the only initial evidence of the baptism. I, along with many others, have received the baptism in the Spirit after receiving the gift of tongues. Others have been baptized in the Spirit prior to getting their prayer language. I do not believe that receiving the gift of tongues is the only way to mark the initial baptism in the Spirit.

Macchia discusses how Pentecostals are increasingly viewing the baptism in the Spirit as a more fluid experience, not necessarily tied to the reception of gifts of the Spirit:

> The older tendency was to see Spirit baptism as a separate reception of the Spirit that functioned as a rite of passage to spiritual fullness and spiritual gifts. What I regard to be a more helpful trend, the tendency now among many Pentecostals is to accent the gift of the Spirit given in regeneration and to view the Pentecostal experience of Spirit baptism as empowerment for witness as a "release" of an already-indwelling Spirit in life. Under the influence of the charismatic movement, the language of fullness tends to be replaced with "release of the Spirit" as an "enhancement" or "renewal" of one's charismatic life.[14]

Macchia, it seems, aligns his views with Assemblies of God thinkers such as Gordon Fee and Gordon Anderson. Anderson, president of North Central University in Minneapolis, argues that not all gifts follow the baptism; only some do. He does not believe—and I agree with him—that a person must speak in tongues to be considered "saved."

Howard Ervin, a Baptist theologian at Oral Roberts University, believes that baptism is necessary for salvation in ontological conversion and that it is effective for empowering Christian ministry in functional baptism.[15] In *Theology with Spirit*, Henry I. Lederle points out that Ervin has unique features in his pneumatology, which he taught at Oral Roberts University for several decades. Lederle lists them as follows:

> The "birthday" of the Church is not Acts 2, but John 20:19–23 (when Jesus breathes on His disciples).
>
> At least for Luke, baptism in the Spirit is synonymous with being filled with the Spirit. The terms are used interchangeably.
>
> Tongues are not sub-rational but supra-rational.
>
> There are seven Pentecosts in the book of Acts: (1) Acts 2:4—Disciples; (2) Acts 4:31—Jewish new believers; (3) Acts 8:14–17—Samaritans; (4) Acts 8:38–39—Ethiopian Eunuch; (5) Acts 9:17—Paul; (6) Acts 10:44–46—Roman; and (7) Acts 19:1–6—Ephesians.
>
> The translation "spiritual gifts" in 1 Corinthians 12 is unfortunate. They are not gifts in the sense of permanent endowments or possessions, but rather manifestations.
>
> Signs are for the world and create faith. Gifts are for the Church and build up the Body.[16]

Ervin is the only scholar, I am aware of, who espouses the "one baptism, one filling" view. He rejects the idea of a refilling based on Acts 4:31. He sees the Spirit as baptizing us into a state of lasting fullness that does not fluctuate. As you will see from my comments in this book, I disagree with Ervin on the "one baptism, one filling" position. I believe that the Bible does teach that multiple fillings or baptisms are possible. In his last publication, *Healing: Sign of the*

Kingdom (2002), Ervin includes a brief chapter on Jesus and the Spirit. Here he makes the distinction between the functional and the ontological. He states that Luke's pneumatology is functional and John's is ontological. The ontological work of the Spirit pertains to the new birth. The functional work is empowering and is inseparable from the phenomena that accompany the baptism in the Spirit, such as tongues, prophecy, healing, etc.[17]

In *A Handbook on Holy Spirit Baptism*, Don Basham discusses his belief that the New Testament describes two baptisms—one in water and one in the Holy Spirit.[18] He goes on to suggest that these baptisms can be separate experiences, one bringing salvation and the other bringing the power of the Holy Spirit, which is important if we want to glorify Jesus by doing His work.[19]

Reverend Tommy Tyson, a United Methodist pastor and evangelist whom many consider a "pioneer in relating Church renewal to the person and work of the Holy Spirit," gives a touching testimony of his Holy Spirit baptism:[20]

> Every time I would question Rufus Moseley about this special presence of Jesus, he would talk about the baptism with the Holy Spirit as a means of coming into union with Jesus. God began creating a great hunger in my heart. I did not know, however, how to go about preparing myself for this baptism by the Holy Spirit. Nevertheless, the Lord slipped in on me.
>
> It happened in the men's Bible class at the church I pastored. The lesson that day was on Pentecost (in the Second Chapter of Acts). The teacher didn't know any more about it experientially than I did. When he finished with the lesson, he turned to me and said, "Pastor, do you have something you'd like to add to this lesson?" I thought to myself, "I have something I'd like to say, but I'd better not let them know it." I wanted to get up and tell these men how desperately I'd been seeking for

the experience that the lesson dealt with. But, when this idea came to my mind, I thought I'd best not speak it, because, if these men, who made up the official body of the church, discovered how inadequate I was, they would lose their respect for me. Then I would no longer have a ministry.

But then, this question came to my mind very forcibly: "Do you want a ministry of your own making, or do you want to be filled with the Spirit of God?" Impulsively, I came up to the lectern and gripped it. It was the most difficult step I have ever had to take: I was willing to make a fool of myself in the eyes of those who had accepted me as their pastor. They loved me very much, and I loved them, so I felt I was sacrificing the most precious thing God had ever given me, and that was the pastorate of this church. In fact, it was so difficult it has made every other step since then relatively easy.

Nevertheless, I told these men how empty I was, how much I really desired and needed what that lesson had dealt with. While I was making a real mess of the whole explanation, God came to my rescue. While I stood before these men, telling them about my need and desire to be filled with the Holy Spirit, God began to fill me. I didn't know what was happening. It was as if wave on wave of power that I had never thought possible began to wash through my heart and mind—my inner being. The first thing of which I became conscious was that I was no longer nearly so concerned about what these men might think about me as I was of a desire to bless them.

This breaking of my fear of public opinion was my first awareness of the baptism of the Holy Spirit. This whole experience came to a climax one evening in the parsonage as I was sharing what had happened to me with my friend Wayne McClain. As we shared together—again, without my knowing what really took place or how it happened—suddenly, from within, without any kind of outward manifestation, there came a revelation of the Lord Jesus Christ Himself—from within me. And, in that moment, the scripture came to my mind and flowed through my lips, "God has made Him to be unto me wisdom and righteousness and sanctification and redemption."

I realized that life is a Person, and His Name is Jesus; that wisdom is a Person and His Name is Jesus; that sanctification is not just gritting your teeth and trying to do it, but it's a person, and His Name is Jesus.

As I understand it, this is what is happening to me in my own life: Jesus being revealed from within.[21]

Chapter 3

THE SCRIPTURAL BASIS FOR THE TRADITIONAL PENTECOSTAL AND EVANGELICAL POSITIONS CONSIDERED

I want now to turn our attention to a consideration of the Scriptures that form the basis of the Pentecostal position on the baptism in the Holy Spirit, keeping in mind both the Evangelical and Catholic understanding of these passages. The passages I am referring to are the following: Acts 2:1-13 (Pentecost); Acts 8:12-17 (Samaria); Acts 9:1-19; 22:16 (Paul); Acts 10:44-46; 11:14-16 (Cornelius); and Acts 19:1-9 (Ephesian disciples). In brief, the Evangelical understanding is that these passages are descriptive of the new birth, which is the entry into the New Covenant at the time of Christian conversion. Simultaneously receiving the baptism in the Holy Spirit at conversion is understood to be the New Testament pattern. The Evangelical belief is that the baptism in the Holy Spirit is an experience simultaneous with being born again. The Catholic understanding of the acts of the Holy Spirit includes new steps in the Church's mission, including baptism of the Gentiles (see Acts 8:26-39; 10:1-48), the missionary journey of Paul and Barnabas (see Acts 13:1-3), and the extension of the mission into Europe (see Acts 16:9-10).[1]

The Scriptures listed above are the primary ones used by Pentecostals in developing their view of the baptism as an experience subsequent to conversion. Traditionally, Pentecostals basically have seen all the personages involved in these passages as already regenerated by the Holy Spirit, having entered into the New Covenant experience of the new birth. However, as noted in the preceding chapter, some Pentecostal scholars are reevaluating this position, allowing for greater diversity as to when, how, and what evidence is connected with the baptism in the Spirit. Let us begin our examination of these Scriptures with Acts 2:1-13.

Acts 2:1-13

These verses describe the disciples' experience in the Upper Room. They were saints of God who were saved by faith, as were Abraham, Isaac, Jacob, David, and other justified believers in the Old Testament. However, they were unique because they lived in the interim time of the ministry of Jesus. The Holy Spirit was prominent in the preparation for Jesus's ministry and upon those who shared in His ministry, but, like John the Baptist, they were still under the Old Covenant. The full experience of the Holy Spirit in an abiding manner was not possible until the New Covenant was established. This did not occur until the Day of Pentecost. Since today we do not live our lives in two dispensations or, put another way, under two covenants, the experience of the 120 disciples cannot be the model for our Christian experience.

Asa Mahan, the successor of Charles Finney as president of Oberlin College whom I consider a pre-Pentecostal, says that we "live in a dispensation of far greater light and knowledge....We have the Old and the New Testament combined."[2]

What are we to make of the 11 disciples who had received the Holy Spirit on the night of the first resurrection as recorded in John 20:22? One cannot argue that Pentecost was their reception of the Spirit. For these disciples, the experience was subsequent to conversion. However, for the remainder of the 120, it appears to have been simultaneous with the regenerating work of the Spirit.

Acts 8:12-17

Acts 8:12 tells us that when the Samaritans "*believed Philip as he preached the good news of the kingdom of God and the name of Jesus Christ, they were baptized, both men and women.*" I want you to note that they believed and then were baptized. Acts 8:14-17 tells us that the Apostles at Jerusalem sent Peter and John to Samaria when they heard that the Samaritans had "*received the word of God*" (Acts 8:14 ESV). Peter and John "*prayed for them that they might receive the Holy Spirit; for he had not yet fallen on any of them, but they had only been baptized in the name of the Lord Jesus. Then they laid their hands on them and they received the Holy Spirit*" (Acts 8:15-17 ESV).

On the surface this passage does seem to teach at least the possibility of the baptism in the Holy Spirit being subsequent to conversion, but questions still remain. Was the apostles' baptism in the Spirit subsequent to conversion, or was this experience their genuine conversion with its correspondent simultaneous baptism in the Holy Spirit?

Dr. James Dunn believes the latter. According to him, Luke means for us to understand that the Samaritans' faith was defective. He gives us two reasons for believing so. First, Luke does not use the usual Greek word for "believe" in reference to the Samaritans. Rather, he uses a different Greek word that means "to believe" in the sense of intellectual assent, which is head knowledge. It also means "to agree intellectually with what has been said." For Dunn, intellectual assent to propositional truth is a defective belief because it does not involve the full commitment of the person. Secondly, he believes that Luke intends to use Simon as a model for the Samaritans. Since Simon's faith was defective, so was the faith of the Samaritans.[3] I find it interesting that this argument of Simon being a model indicating that the Samaritan's faith was defective is not later applied to Apollos and the Ephesian disciples. Consistency would demand that this model idea would prove the Ephesian disciples were really already Christian disciples like Apollos. Dunn, however, is not consistent in applying his arguments when they do not fit his system.

Michael Green, however, has noted that the word Luke uses for "believe" is used in other Bible passages for the saving kind of belief.[4] Therefore, Green finds Dunn's argument weak. I, too, believe this is the weakest point in Dunn's book. Here, the Pentecostal perspective of subsequence is the most natural meaning of the text in its context.

Asa Mahan, while agreeing with the Pentecostal perspective of subsequense, believes that the most striking characteristic of the apostles' baptism was power. He also suggests that the apostles were marked with boldness and courage following their baptism under the new dispensation.[5] I believe that God, in His sovereignty, withheld the experience of the Spirit coming "upon" the disciples so as to await the arrival of the apostles from Jerusalem in order that they might see firsthand God's acceptance of non-Jews into the infant Church. This was one of the purposes of visible manifestations of the Holy Spirit, especially tongues, in the early days of the Church. They were visible signs of God's breaking down prejudicial barriers and accepting all men and women into the Church on the basis of repentance and faith alone. Though tongues were not specifically mentioned in this passage, it is clear that some visible manifestation occurred. The Bible explicitly says, *"When Simon saw that the Spirit was given…"* (Acts 8:18). Some possible manifestations that Simon might have witnessed include shaking, trembling, staggering as if drunk, crying, laughing, and being slain in the Spirit. I personally believe that if tongues were the primary manifestation, Luke would have stated so in the Book of Acts. I believe that the Holy Spirit knew that if the manifestation was clearly identified that the human tendency would be to allow only as valid the manifestations recorded in the New Testament thus limiting the sovereignty of God in His various ways of moving upon people.

Acts 10:44-46; 11:14-16

Now let us look at the story of Cornelius. Pentecostals see Cornelius as already saved and the experience of tongues at Peter's preaching as his baptism in the Spirit, which was subsequent to his time of conversion. I do not agree. It is true that Cornelius was a religious man. According to the Bible, he was *"a devout man who feared God with all his household, gave alms liberally to the people, and prayed constantly to God"* (Acts 10:2, ESV). Cornelius was a "God-fearer." This title was used for those Gentiles who embraced the moral law and worshiped the One God of Judaism. He, too, was justified by faith under the Old Covenant. His experience, however, was not that of the new birth under the New Covenant. Cornelius himself tells Peter that the angel had directed him to *"send to Joppa and bring Simon called Peter; he will declare to you a message by which you will be saved…"* (Acts 11:13-14 ESV). This clearly teaches that Cornelius and his household received their conversion during Peter's visit and his preaching to them.

Again tongues were given to verify to the Apostle Peter the legitimacy of people's conversion and acceptance by God. Another barrier had been torn down: not only was God accepting Jews and Samaritans, but now He was accepting Gentile God-fearers into the Christian faith and Church.

This passage does not fit the Pentecostal system, just as the Samaritan passage does not fit the Evangelical system. God does not fit His work into either the Pentecostal or the Evangelical position on this subject. Rather, He is a God of diversity who is revealed through both positions.

Acts 19:17

Finally, let us consider the case of the disciples at the city of Ephesus. The Pentecostals find here a classic text that seems to teach the baptism in the Holy Spirit as an experience subsequent to conversion. They see these disciples as Christians but do not believe the disciples received the baptism in the Holy Spirit. Their thinking is based on the King James Version of Acts 19:2. It reads, *"Have ye received the Holy Ghost since ye believed?"* (Acts 19:2 KJV). Dunn regards this as an inaccurate translation that has been corrected in the modern translations. According to him, the proper translation reads, "Did you receive the Holy Spirit *when* you believed?"[6] Not being a Greek scholar myself, when I first read Dunn's book, his argument convinced me. Since that time, the New International Version has been printed. In its footnote to Acts 19:2 it gives "after" as a possibility, rather than "when." I realize now that the modern translations have been completed since the beginning of the Pentecostal movement. Because almost all of the translators were not Pentecostal in their beliefs and experiences, their theology affected their translation. Instead of allowing for both possibilities, which would acknowledge that either "when" or "after" can both accurately reflect the meaning of the Greek work, they gave only one option.

I thought it would be very interesting to see how this verse has been translated into other languages, as well as English, prior to 1901, the birth of Pentecostalism. I found this so interesting that I called the library of The Southern Baptist Theological Seminary and asked them to send me the photocopies of English translations of this passage that would have been written prior to 1901. I received photocopies of four of the oldest English translations. They were written in the 1500s, prior to the King James Version. All of them translated the word "since" rather than "when."

Dunn believes Paul's question to the disciples at Ephesus, *"Did you receive the Holy Spirit when you believed?"* was really a test to see if these men were Christians or not (Acts 19:2). The apostolic preaching as recorded in Acts always mentioned the Holy Spirit; note Peter's Pentecostal sermon in the second chapter of Acts. How could these men have accepted the gospel of Jesus Christ and not have heard of the Holy Spirit? I believe it would have been very unlikely. Much of the Church in today's world, however, would find this omission of the Holy Spirit commonplace.

According to Acts 19:3-5, men had been baptized by John the Baptist but had not received Christian baptism. We know that Luke did not reserve the word "disciple" for Christian disciples only, for in his Gospel he speaks of John the Baptist's disciples (see Luke 7:18). Dunn believes that they were the disciples of John the Baptist and that they received the Holy Spirit at the time of their conversion, which occurred during their water baptism and Paul's laying on of hands.[7] In fact, there are five accounts in the Book of Acts where people received baptism in the Holy Spirit, and in three of those accounts, the people were ministered to through the laying on of hands.[8] Tongues were present at the time of conversion-initiation and not subsequent to it. It should be taken into account that the term "conversion-initiation" allows for the concept of subsequence from a Pentecostal perspective because Pentecostals would not see baptism in water as necessary for conversion, though it would certainly be a part of initiation into the local church.

I believe that Dunn is correct in thinking that these followers were not yet Christians when Paul met them. As I see it, Paul baptized them, and they became Christians. Subsequent to their baptism they were filled with the Spirit: when Paul laid his hands upon them, the Holy Spirit *came on them* and they spoke in tongues and prophesied. I believe this was subsequent to their conversion— but with only a small amount of time between the baptism and the laying on of hands. This verse, along with the Samaritan passage, forms the biblical basis for the early Church to see the baptism in the Spirit and the laying on of hands as part of the conversion-initiation process that Dunn mentioned. (For Catholics, the justification and regeneration occur at water baptism; the Spirit regenerates the person, giving them eternal life). But the fullness of the Spirit coming upon them occurs with the laying on of hands with prayer for the Holy Spirit to fill the person. John Wesley saw justification as coming by faith, not as dependent on this second work of grace. But for him, the full assurance of salvation came with the filling of the Spirit—sanctification or baptism in the Spirit. Wesley was strongly impacted by the Church Fathers, as we will later see.

One should not hide behind the supposedly "correct" translation of Scripture and precise biblical language pertaining to the baptism in the Holy Spirit, without experiencing the reality of the baptism in the Spirit. Pentecostals and Charismatics today, like the earliest Methodists, and later their spiritual forerunners in the Holiness movement and the earliest Methodists, are to be praised for their emphasis on the experience of the Spirit. In my discussions with Dr. Jon Ruthven, he has noted that it seems like in Acts, Luke is unaware of any problem of "subsequence" (the Spirit coming after conversion). Rather, Luke's only interest is to see the mission of Jesus fulfilled by the baptism of the Holy Spirit. Luke is not interested in *when* one receives the Spirit, only *that* one receives the Spirit, because the only true goal of the Christian experience is to be a Spirit-filled disciple. Ruthven further notes that God can and does send His Spirit on a continuum of experiences ranging from "general revelation," regeneration, etc., all the way through the baptism in the Holy Spirit, which is the "heavenly gift, a taste of the powers of the age to come" (see Heb. 6:4-5). Ruthven points out that in the Bible, the Spirit is seen overwhelmingly as revelation, prophecy, and power and is not limited to the *ordo salutis*—the normal order of salvation (see 1 Cor. 12).

R. A. Torrey, in his book *The Baptism with the Holy Spirit*, states that "a comparison of Acts 2:39 with Luke 24:49, as well as Acts 1:4, 5; 2:33; and 2:38 with Acts 10:45 and 11:15,16, shows that *the promise* and *the gift of the Holy Ghost* both refer to the baptism with the Holy Spirit. The result of the baptism with the Spirit that was most noticeable and essential was a convincing, convicting and converting power. (Acts 2:4,37,41; 4:8-13,31,33; 9:17,20-22.)"[9]

Presently, I am reflecting upon my study in this area. As I do so, I recall Roman Catholic Cardinal Léon-Joseph Suenens's language about "appropriating" the reality of our potential in Christ. In a similar theological manner, Arnold Bittlinger, a German Lutheran Charismatic professor of Theology, believes:

> Every Christian has been baptized in both [water and spirit] or he or she is not a Christian in the full sense of the word. In baptism one receives potentially everything one will ever receive in Christ. But God's purpose in baptism must be actualized through the appropriation of its potential in the life of the individual Christian.[10]

Both Suenens the Catholic and Bittlinger the Lutheran are attempting to relate the experience of regeneration and justification and the baptism in the Spirit as the same experience occurring at the same time. Most denominations other than Holiness and Pentecostalism attempt to relate these two experiences as happening at the same time, while the Holiness and Pentecostal denominations see them as two distinct experiences happening at two distinct times. Not all Catholics attempt to keep them together as Suenens does.

Again, from the non-Charismatic Southern Baptist professor Dr. Robert Culpepper:

> It is better to speak incorrectly of a second blessing or a second Pentecost and lay hold of the reality of new life in Christ than to let the soundness of our doctrine rob us of its substance.[11]

One of the great New Testament scholars of our day, Dr. Gordon Fee, has a wonderful chapter on the baptism in the Holy Spirit in his book *Gospel and Spirit: Issues in New Testament Hermeneutics*. In particular, Chapter 7, entitled "Baptism in the Holy Spirit: The Issue of Separability and Subsequence," is very helpful in healing the divide between Evangelicals and Pentecostals. In this section, Fee states:

> The purpose of this present essay is to open the question of separability and subsequence once again, and (1) to suggest that there is in fact very little biblical support for the traditional Pentecostal position on this matter, but (2) to argue further that this is of little consequence to the doctrine of the baptism in the Holy Spirit, either as to the validity of the experience itself or its articulation."[12]

He goes on to say:

> What I hope to show in the rest of this essay is that the Pentecostals are generally right on target biblically as to their *experience* of the Spirit. Their difficulties arose from the attempt to defend it biblically at the wrong point.[13]

I find myself in total agreement with Fee's position on this matter. In particular, I agree with him when he writes:

> In thus arguing, as a New Testament scholar, against some cherished Pentecostal interpretations, I have in no sense abandoned what is essential to Pentecostalism. I have only tried to point out some inherent flaws in some of our historic understanding of the texts. The essential matter, after all, is neither subsequence nor tongues, but the Spirit himself as a dynamic, empowering presence; and there seems to me to be little question that our way of initiation into that—through an experience of Spirit baptism—has biblical validity. Whether all *must* go that route seems to me to be more moot; but in any case, the Pentecostal experience itself can be defended on exegetical grounds as a thoroughly biblical phenomenon....*I think it is fair to note that if there is one thing that differentiates the early church from its twentieth-century*

counterpart it is the level of awareness and experience of the presence and power of the Holy Spirit. Ask any number of people of today from all sectors of Christendom to define or describe Christian conversion or Christian life, *and the most noticeable feature of that definition would be its general lack of emphasis on the active, dynamic role of the Spirit.*

It is precisely the opposite in the New Testament. The Spirit is no mere addendum. Indeed, he is the *sine qua non, the essential ingredient, of Christian life.* Nor is he a mere datum of theology; rather, he is *experienced* as a powerful presence in their lives.[14]

By looking at the biblical texts to see reception of the Spirit as something that was part and parcel of their conversion experience Fee sets out to indicate that this reception was inclusive of receiving the Spirit along with visible manifestations of His presence.

Indeed, it was the Pentecostals' ability to read the New Testament existence so correctly, along with their frustration over the less-than-adequate norm of anemia that they experienced in their own lives and in the Church around them, that led to seeking for the New Testament experience in the first place. The question, of course, is, if that was the norm, what happened to the Church in the succeeding generations? It is in pursuit of that question that an understanding of the Pentecostal experience as separate and subsequent lies.[15]

Fee raises the questions as to whether or not the Pentecostal experience must be seen as without biblical precedent because it does not fit the biblical pattern, or whether Pentecostals need to reinterpret the Bible to fit their experience. To both these questions he answers, "No!" How then are we to let the Bible speak clearly what it says while also validating the Pentecostals' experience of the Spirit? He writes:

> On the one hand, the typical Evangelical or Reformed exegete who disallows a separate and subsequent experience simply must hide his or her head in the sand, ostrich like, to deny the reality—the biblical reality—of what has happened to so many Christians. On the other hand, the Pentecostal must be wary of reforming the biblical data to fit his or her own experience. The solution, it seems to me, lies in two areas: (1) An examination of the components of Christian conversion as they emerge in the New Testament, and (2) an analysis of what happened to Christian experience once the Church entered into a second and third generation of believers.

Without belaboring any of the points in detail, it seems to me that the components of Christian conversion that emerge from the New Testament data are five:

1. The actual conviction of sin, with the consequent drawing of the individual to Christ. This, all agree, is the prior work of the Holy Spirit that *leads* to conversion.

2. The application of the atonement in the person's life, including the forgiveness of the past, the canceling of the debt of sin. I would tend to put repentance here as a part of the response to the prior grace of God, which is also effected by the Spirit.

3. The regenerating work of the Holy Spirit that gives new birth, that brings forth the new creation.

4. The empowerment for life, with openness to gifts and the miraculous, plus obedience to mission. This is the component that Pentecostals want to make

subsequent to numbers *1, 2, 3,* and the Protestant tradition wants to limit simply to fruit and growth, but tends at times seemingly to omit altogether.

5. The believer's response to all this is baptism in water, the offering of oneself back to God for life and service in His new-age community, the church. This act obviously carries with it the rich symbolism of elements 2 and 3 (forgiveness and regeneration), but in itself effects neither.

> The crucial item in all of this for the early church was the work of the Spirit; and element *4,* the dynamic empowering dimension with gifts, miracles, and evangelism (along with fruit and growth), was a normal part of their expectation and experience.[16]

Fee points out that the problem is that point 4, the dynamic reality of the Spirit, became lost in the subsequent history of the Church. A condition arose that was very different from the experiences of the New Testament believers. Christian life came to consist of conversion without empowerment, baptism without obedience, and grace without love. Indeed, the whole Calvinist-Arminian debate is predicated on this reality—that people can be in the Church but evidence little or nothing of the work of the Spirit in their lives.[17] Few would argue that this is not the case, but how did this situation develop? According to Fee there are two main reasons for this development:

> The first is that the New Testament was written to first-generation Christians who were baptized as adults, thus the issue of second and third generations wasn't addressed. The conversions for the succeeding generations of those who grew up in Christian homes would not be so dramatic or life changing. The dynamic experiential nature of the conversion experience would be the first to go.[18]

The second and most devastating reason was the connection between water baptism and the reception of the Spirit. With the eventual acceptance of the practice of infant baptism the dynamic experiential nature of conversion was lost. This would prove to be the case for most of Christian history, but it was not the situation in the Bible. All the pietistic movements since the Montanists to the Toronto Blessing must be understood as a reaction to the sub-normal life of the Christians in the Church in comparison to the life in the Spirit that is depicted in the Bible.[19]

It is precisely out of such a background that one is to understand the Pentecostal movement with its deep dissatisfaction with life in Christ without life in the Spirit and their subsequent experience of a mighty baptism in the Spirit. *If their timing was off as far as the biblical norm was concerned, their experience itself was not.* What they were recapturing for the Church was the empowering dimension of life in the Spirit as the normal Christian life.

That this experience was for them usually a separate experience in the Holy Spirit and subsequent to their conversion is in itself probably irrelevant. Given their place in the history of the church, how else might it have happened? Thus the Pentecostal should probably not make a virtue out of necessity. At the same time, neither should others deny the validity of such experience on biblical grounds, unless, as some do, they wish to deny the reality of such an empowering dimension of life in the Spirit altogether. *But such a denial, I would argue, is actually an exegeting not of the biblical texts but of one's own experience in this later point in church history and a making of that experience normative.* I for one like the biblical norm better; at this point the Pentecostals have the New Testament clearly on their side.[20]

When all of the quotes in this chapter are taken together, they can be summarized as follows: if the Book of Acts has a "pattern" for when one receives the Spirit, it's that there is no pattern, except that it follows a "preparation," or repentance and baptism (according to John the Baptist in Matthew 3:11, Mark 1:4, Luke 3:3, and Acts 2:38). And even this pattern is not regularly followed in Acts. In Acts 10, Cornelius and his household experience the baptism of the Holy Spirit before conversion and repentance. In the New Testament, especially in Acts, there is no real interest in the question of *when* one receives the Spirit; the focus is only *that* one receives Him, because as we shall see, this is Jesus's prime goal.

Furthermore, the Pentecostals' view of the baptism in the Holy Spirit as evidenced by speaking in tongues as an experience subsequent to their conversion is based upon weak biblical support. The Evangelicals have done an even greater injustice to the Bible by almost totally missing the nature of the Christian life as vibrant, dynamic, supernatural animation in the Holy Spirit. The necessity for a subsequent experience in the Spirit is not determined by biblical texts but rather by one's place in Christian history, because for the majority of people, their baptism in the Spirit follows their conversion.

I believe that Evangelicals owe a great debt to the Pentecostals. Along with the Charismatics, Pentecostals have been virtually alone in emphasizing that the charismata, or grace gifts, are still the birthright of the Church. They have rejected the traditional Protestant and the more recent dispensational views that the gifts of the Spirit disappeared with either the death of the Apostles or the canonization of the New Testament. Today, many within the Evangelical camp are listening to their Pentecostal and Charismatic brothers. What excites me now is the possibility of Evangelicals becoming open to expecting and experiencing the gifts of the Holy Spirit without having to identify with the Pentecostal interpretation of the baptism in the

Holy Spirit or what I believe has been a legalistic, pharisaic attitude within much of Pentecostalism.

In a 2015 interview with *Christianity Today*, Southern Baptist pastor, author, and theologian J. D. Greear says:

> I had always been a little frustrated, because it just seemed like people in the Bible had a fundamentally different relationship with God than my own. There was a hollowness in my spiritual life. God was more a doctrine than a person. I also felt crushed by the amount of stuff that needed to be done in the world. There was always one more orphan, always one more unreached people group. I began to discover that an understanding of our relationship with the Holy Spirit helps to soothe these anxieties. Instead of saying, "Look at all that God needs me to do for him," the Spirit reminds us to say, "Look at what God is empowering me to do."[21]

One cannot deny the genuine accounts of the "sign gifts" in operation today. In particular, the Charismatics have left the "sawdust trail" and have entered the graduate departments of our universities. Much of what they say about the gifts is well balanced, biblical, and usually more accurate than Evangelical interpretations. We must, as God does, look at the motive behind this legalism within Pentecostalism. I believe it is motivated by a misunderstanding of Christ's idea of holiness coupled with a deep love for Him. Therefore, let us be temperate in our condemnation of this legalism. In reality, it seems to be passing away. In addition, many Evangelical groups at the turn of the century similarly evinced this sort of legalism.

Furthermore, let us not forget the multiple examples of great men and women of God who spoke of an experience, call it what you may, subsequent to conversion that radically changed their lives and made them victorious—people like John Wesley, George Whitefield, Charles Finney, Andrew Murray, A. B. Simpson, A. J.

Gordon, D. L. Moody, R. A. Torrey, Evan Roberts, F. F. Bosworth, Billy Sunday, Billy Graham, Rolland and Heidi Baker, Bill Johnson, Che Ahn, Georgian and Winnie Banov, John and Carol Arnott, and myself and my wife DeAnne. Actually, a high percentage of the key history makers in the Church have had such an encounter.

I personally sense my inadequacy in the area of ministry and relationship to the Holy Spirit. David (Paul) Yonggi Cho and the late John Wimber have emphasized our need to be intimate with the Holy Spirit. Mike Bickle calls this "developing a secret history in God."[22] This is the deep need of the Church today.

Chapter 4

Baptism in the Holy Spirit According to Early Church Fathers and Early Church Historians

The history of the Church is replete with examples of Holy Spirit baptism. These historical baptisms are part of the rich foundation upon which the Church stands, giving witness to what God has done among His people and hope for what He will do now and in the age to come. Hebrews 6:5 refers to those *"who have tasted the goodness of the word of God and the power of the age to come"* (NLT). As believers we are privileged to receive power now from God, which is but a foretaste of a full manifestation of the Kingdom of God that is to come (see Heb. 2:4). This unfolding of biblical eschatology—this "now and not yet" aspect of our current state—is a place of holy tension where all believers should desire to dwell.

In this chapter we will turn our attention to what the Church Fathers and some of the early Church historians have said about the subject of baptism in the Holy Spirit.

Theophilus of Antioch (ca. 169–183)

Theophilus, a former pagan turned Christian apologist who served as bishop of Antioch from A.D. 169 to 183, wrote an extensive apologetic to his pagan friend Autolycus in defense of Christianity. In an effort to help his friend understand the meaning of the name "Christian," Theophilus proposed that "the air and all that is under heaven is in a certain sort anointed by light and spirit; and are you unwilling to be anointed with the oil of God? Wherefore we are called Christians on this account, because we are anointed with the oil of God."[1] Here, Theophilus is making reference to the anointing with oil for the Holy Spirit at baptism and the laying on of hands for the Holy Spirit that prepares and empowers the Christian to fight the good fight in spiritual warfare.

Tertullian (ca. 155–240)

Tertullian, one of the great theologians of the second century and a prolific writer in the Church, lived in Carthage, a city in modern-day Tunisia. He wrote an entire book on baptism in the Holy Spirit in which he described the process of coming up from the baptismal waters and being anointed with the blessed unction based on the custom established by Moses when he anointed Aaron for priesthood with oil out of a horn (see Lev. 8:12).[2] This passage in Leviticus indicates that in Moses's day it was believed to be very important—even part of the baptismal ritual—to lay hands on those just baptized, anoint them with oil, and pray for them to be filled with the Holy Spirit. In this ritual we see the faith of the early Church regarding baptism. Baptism wasn't only about coming to Christ and repenting; it was also about Christ coming to the newly baptized in the filling of the Spirit, which was expected at baptism with the laying on of hands. This ties together even closer the fourth and fifth elementary teachings of Hebrews 6:1-2: the doctrine of baptism and the laying on of hands.

Both the act of baptizing with water and the anointing with oil accompanied by prayer for one to be filled with the Holy Spirit were two parts of one experience, or what Dunn calls "conversion-initiation."[3] In passing it is also important to note that after the person was baptized there was not only the laying on of hands, but there was also a prayer for deliverance for the newly baptized person. Regarding water baptism and its relationship to Spirit baptism, Tertullian comments, "I do not mean to say that we obtain the Holy Spirit in the water, but having been cleansed in the water, we are being prepared under the angel for the Holy Spirit."[4] Tertullian instructed catechumens preparing for baptism, "Therefore, you blessed ones, for whom the grace of God is waiting, when you come up from the most sacred bath of the new birth, when you spread out your hands for the first time in your mother's house with your brethren, ask your Father, ask your Lord, for the special gift of His inheritance, the distributed charisms....Ask, He says, and you shall receive."[5]

Clement of Alexandria (ca. 150–215)

Clement was born in Athens, Greece, circa A.D. 150 and died in Jerusalem, Israel, around A.D. 215. He was a Christian theologian who taught in Alexandria at the Catechetical School. According to him, "The Apostle John delivered a young man to the care of a bishop who baptized him, and afterwards he sealed him with the Lord's signature as a safe and perfect guard."[6] "The Lord's seal" and "the Lord's signature" were terms used by early Christians to refer to the filling of the Holy Spirit. The filling of the Holy Spirit was called "the sealing of the Spirit."

Origen of Alexandria (ca. 185–254)

Origen was born in Alexandria, Egypt, in A.D. 185 and died in Tyre, Lebanon, in A.D. 254. He was a pupil of Clement of Alexandria. He became one of the great theologians of his time. In referring to baptism, Origen writes that oil is of holy doctrine, and he states:

"So then, when someone receives this oil that the saint makes use of, that is, the Scripture that lays down how he ought to be baptized in the name of the Father and of the Son and of the Holy Spirit [cf. Matt 28:19], and by making a few changes he anoints someone and says some such thing as: You are no longer a catechumen, you have attained to 'the washing of the second birth'...."[7]

Pope Urban I (d. A.D. 230)

Pope Urban I was one of the earliest bishops of Rome, from A.D. 222 to 230. He believed that faithful people should receive the baptism of the Spirit "by imposition of the bishop's hands."[8]

St. Cyprian (ca. 200–258)

St. Cyprian, bishop of Carthage, North Africa, born around A.D. 200 and martyred in A.D. 258, was the most famous Latin Christian theologian until Jerome and Augustine. In writing about Philip's experience at Samaria as recorded in Acts 8, he notes, "The faithful in Samaria had already obtained baptism; only that which was wanting Peter and John supplied, by prayer and imposition of hands, to the end the Holy Ghost might be poured upon them."[9] Cyprian believed that prayers for new converts to receive the filling of the Holy Spirit were necessary "*to complete man's sanctification.*"[10] Cyprian employs the phrase "the Lord's fullness" as an expression of being filled or baptized in the Holy Spirit. He wrote to Cornelius, the bishop of Rome, that "those whom they would have to be safe against the corruptions of their adversaries, they should arm them with the guards and defenses of the *Lord's fullness.*"[11]

Eusebius (ca. 263–339)

Eusebius was a Greek historian and the father of Church history. He was also an apologist for the faith. He was the bishop of Caesarea Maritima from A.D. 314 until his death. Eusebius tells how Novatian, a Roman priest and prolific author, was censured by Bishop Cornelius because, although he had been baptized while he was sick, he had not had hands laid upon him *for the filling of the Holy Spirit*. When Novatian recovered, he did not have hands laid upon him. Eusebius explained that "he was not consigned with the Lord's signature by the hands of the bishop, which *having not obtained, how can he be supposed to have received the Holy Ghost?*"[12] This quote reveals that the rule of the Church in the latter half of the third century was still that *all baptized converts should be prayed for that they might receive the Holy Ghost*. The Church believed the Spirit was *with* the new believer once he or she had been baptized and regenerated, but only came *into* the person after the imposition of hands and prayer for the person to be filled. In the Western Church, or what would become the Roman Catholic Church, the prayer for filling with the Holy Spirit was offered by the bishop. In the Eastern (later the Orthodox) Church, the prayers could be prayed by any priest. Yet in the Bible we find God using Ananias, someone who doesn't appear to have any church office, to pray for Saul to recover his sight and be filled with the Spirit.

Firmilian (d. ca. 269)

Firmilian, the bishop of Caesarea Mazaca from A.D. 232 until his death circa A.D. 269, and St. Ambrose were the first to use the word "confirm" for the filling of the Holy Spirit connected with the water baptismal rite. This was based upon the Latin word *confirmatio*, and was in reference to Paul "confirming" the 12 disciples in Ephesus, as the Latin text reads, and is also drawn from Second Corinthians 1:21-22.[13] The writers of this time believed that "stablishing," "anointing," and "sealing" all referred to being filled with the Holy Spirit. The term "confirmation" (confirm) began to be used for the imposition of hands and prayer for the filling of the Holy Spirit. This usage began about the time of St. Ambrose, who lived from approximately A.D. 340 to 397.

Pope Melchiades (d. A.D. 314)

Pope Melchiades (or Miltiades) was the first pope to see the end of the Roman persecution of Christians. In his letter to the bishop of Spain, he points out how important confirmation is for the new believer. Confirmation as used here refers to the time the newly baptized person is anointed and has hands laid on him or her for the prayer to be filled with the Holy Spirit. From what Melchiades says, it appears that this experience was not thought of as a ritual without power but rather as a mystery of empowerment that went all the way back to the practice of the apostles: "What does the mystery of confirmation profit me *after* the mystery of baptism? *Certainly we did not receive all in our baptism, if after the washing we want something of another kind....*Therefore, the Holy Spirit is the guardian of our regeneration in Christ, He is Comforter, and He is the defender."[14] If it were only a ritual of the Church that did not convey real experiential power, Melchiades' words would lose their power and import.

Melchiades believed regeneration in baptism was sufficient to prepare us for death but that the living needed "the auxiliaries of confirmation."[15] In other words, for him, the experiential benefits of being filled or baptized in the Holy Spirit were not optional; they were necessary. Again, this would not be said if confirmation, i.e., baptism in the Holy Spirit, was a mere datum of theology or liturgical practice. These types of statements reveal that the baptism in the Holy Spirit was more than theological; it was phenomenological-experiential. Real power came upon the people, enabling them to fight the good fight of faith and to obey the commissions of Jesus to heal the sick, cast out demons, raise the dead, and cleanse the lepers—real power to establish justice, bring good news to the poor, care for the widows and the orphans, and visit those in prison; real power to refrain from denying the faith under persecution. Christianity was granted legal status just one year before Melchiades died. Throughout the majority of his life he would have known of Roman persecution of Christians.

Eusebius Emesenus (ca. 300–360)

Eusebius Emesenus was born in what is today Edessa, Turkey, in A.D. 300. He died in A.D. 360 in Antioch. He was the bishop of Emesa (today's Hems, Syria) from 341 to 359. Similar to Melchiades, he believed that the laying on of hands confirmed that one is born again in Christ. He, too, used the metaphor of a believer becoming a warrior in baptism when given the weapons with which to fight through the imposition of hands in confirmation.[16]

St. Gregory Nazianzen (A.D. 329–389)

St. Gregory, also known as Gregory the Theologian, was a fourth-century archbishop of Constantinople. He presided over the Second Ecumenical Council in 381. In regard to the filling or baptism in the Holy Spirit that was conferred through the imposition of hands and prayer, which was part of the baptismal liturgy of the early Church, Gregory stated the following: "We therefore call it a seal or signature, as being a guard and custody to us, and a sign of the Lord's dominion over us."[17] This seal or signature is a reference to the filling with the Spirit that is part of the baptismal rite—at least initially. Later, priests began performing the rites of baptism and confirmation at different times, especially as infant baptism increased in popularity.

St. Ambrose (A.D. 337–397)

St. Ambrose became the bishop of Milan in 374. He was one of the greatest and most important leaders of the Church in the fourth century and considered one of the four original doctors of the Church. It was through his teaching and preaching that St. Augustine came to the faith, leaving his pagan religion. He considered the reception of the Holy Spirit through the laying on of hands and prayer a type of spiritual seal that remained after baptism, also using the term "confirm" for such a sealing by impartation.[18]

St. John Chrysostom (A.D. 347–407)

St. John Chrysostom, ordained as a deacon in Antioch in 381, served there for 16 years before being appointed archbishop of Constantinople in 397. Although the church in Antioch was determined that such a popular deacon as Chrysostom not be "stolen" from them, St. John looked upon his appointment as Archbishop of Constantinople as the providence of God and accepted the new position.

St. John believed that to receive power from above, one must receive it through the Holy Spirit. His writings reveal that this belief was in reference to Peter and John coming to Samaria to pray for the Holy Spirit to come upon those Philip had baptized. It is clear from these passages that St. John did not believe one was filled with the Holy Spirit at the moment of regeneration but rather afterwards, at the laying on of hands and prayer. Commenting on Hebrews 6:1-2, he writes, "To be baptized into the faith of Christ, and be made worthy of the gift of the Spirit, Who is given by imposition of hands...."[19]

St. Jerome (A.D. 347–420)

St. Jerome is perhaps best known for translating the Bible from Greek into Latin, a translation that came to be known as the Vulgate. When Jerome was asked why people who were baptized did not receive the Holy Spirit except by having hands laid upon them and receiving prayer, he would direct the questioner to the Book of Acts stating, "The consent of the whole Christian world in this article ought to prevail as a commandment." Jerome was referring to the fact that the entire Christian world at that time believed that one received the Holy Spirit when bishops or elders prayed for them with the laying on of hands.[20]

St. Cyril (A.D. 378–444)

When St. Cyril was the patriarch of Alexandria, it was at the height of its importance as a major city in the Roman Empire. He was a key leader at the Council of Ephesus, where Nestorius was deposed, in 431. St. Cyril believed that when Jesus was baptized in the river of Jordan, He ascended out of the water with the Holy Spirit upon Him. Moreover, he believed that when a person was baptized with the Holy Spirit, it was as if armor was put on him or her to withstand the enemy's powers.[21]

St. Augustine (A.D. 354–430)

St. Augustine is considered by many scholars to be the most important figure in Western Christianity. In 396 he became bishop of Hippo, an office he held until his death in 430.

St. Augustine wrote of believers speaking in tongues after the Holy Spirit came upon them. He recognized that tongues were especially important in order to take the Gospel of God to other nations and languages. The Church, at this time, believed in the remission of sins and gifts of the Holy Spirit, to which Augustine attests when he writes: "In the Church truly in which was the Holy Ghost, were both brought to pass, that is, both the remission of sins, and the receiving of the gift."[22]

St. Augustine had much to say about the baptism in the Holy Spirit and the charisms of the Spirit. Speaking of water baptism, he cautions, "We must not think that those who have received a valid baptism have also automatically (*continuo*) received the Holy Spirit."[23] In its proper context, Augustine's quote can be understood as referring to the baptism in the Holy Spirit.

Pope Leo I (A.D. 390–461)

Pope Leo I, also known as St. Leo the Great, believed that people who returned to the Church should have hands laid upon them to receive the Holy Spirit.[24]

St. Simeon the New Theologian (A.D. 949–1022)

Simeon is considered the fourth most important theologian of the Orthodox Church. For Simeon the Holy Spirit was the principle of all spiritual life." Simeon, like Dr. Jon Ruthven today, believed that the incarnation was "accomplished by the power of the Holy Spirit."[25]

Simeon's theology went a step further than the position Wesley would later hold—that one is justified by faith apart from experiencing the powerful presence of God in sanctification or baptism in the Holy Spirit. (For Wesley, these two terms referred to the same experience.) Wesley believed that what gives a person full assurance of salvation is the subsequent experience of the Spirit. Simeon, on the other hand, explains:

> Our salvation is not to be found only in the baptism of water. It is also to be found in the Spirit; just as it is not exclusively in the bread and wine of communion that we are given forgiveness of our sins and enabled to share in life....May no one venture to say: 'Since holy baptism, I have received Christ and I possess him'. Let him, on the contrary, learn that not all those who are baptized received Christ through baptism, but only those who are strengthened in faith and (who reach) Perfect knowledge, or those who have been prepared by purification and are therefore well disposed to come to baptism. (*Ethical Treatise X (129, 273, 283)*).
>
> Those who received your baptism in early infancy and who have throughout their lives lived unworthily of you will be more severely condemned than those who have not been baptized....O Savior, you gave repentance for a second purification, and you established as its end the grace of the Spirit that we first received at baptism, since it is not only 'by water' that grace comes, according to your words, but rather 'by the Spirit,' in

the invocation of the Trinity. Since we were baptized as unknowing children and as beings who were still imperfect, we receive grace also very imperfectly (*Hymn LV, 28-29 (129, 255ff); cf. 61ff (p. 259)).*[26]

Simeon must not be understood as a pre-Protestant who is rejecting a sacramental system, for he elsewhere makes statements that would give Luther and other Protestants cause to be concerned. Regarding negative statements about false faith, Simeon states:

> Once again I find myself grappling with those who say that they have the Spirit of God in an unconscious manner and who imagine that they have possessed him since their baptism. They may be convinced that they have this treasure, but they do not recognize its importance. I have to deal with those who confess that they felt nothing at their baptism and who believe that the gift of God has dwelt in them in an unconscious and intangible manner and that it is still subsisting even now in that way in their souls.
>
> If someone were to say that each one of us believers receives and possesses the Spirit without knowing it or being conscious of it, he would be blaspheming by making Christ lie when he said: 'In Him there will be a spring of water welling up to eternal life' (John 4:14) and: 'He who believes in me, out of his heart shall flow rivers of living water' (7:38) (*Ethical Treatise X* (129, 297)).[27]

Congar, in his assessment of the issues of salvation and faith and salvation and the sacraments, summarizes what he believed was Simeon's position regarding both:

> Just as the sacrament alone is insufficient in itself, so too is faith, which is mere belief, faith based on catechetical formulae. Faith calls for works, and these are above all works of 'repentance' (the baptism of tears, which plays such an important part in Simeon's teaching) and works

of effective charity. It is then that the fruits of the Spirit follow, as the signs of his indwelling (*Ethical Treatise IX (129, 241)*). For Simeon, then, possession of the Spirit and animation by the Spirit were normally the object of experience. This is an essential part of his teaching.[28]

Conclusion

Fifteen centuries after Theophilus of Antioch proposed that believers need the laying on of hands that brings the Holy Spirit in order to live an empowered life, Jeremy Taylor (1613–1667), a cleric in the Church of England who eventually became a bishop in Ireland and vice-chancellor of the University of Dublin, echoed this belief as part of his *Chrisis teleiōtikē*, a discourse of confirmation he wrote during his tenure in Ireland to instruct clergy and laity. Taylor's instruction includes an explanation of how the laying on of hands for prayer for the Holy Spirit became known as a type of "sacrament of chrism."[29] Now, some 350 years after Taylor we find the same theology of baptism of the Holy Spirit echoing through the Church.

With this brief glimpse into the views, beliefs, and practices of some of the early Church fathers and historians regarding baptism in the Holy Spirit, let us continue to turn an eye to the past as we examine baptism in the Holy Spirit from both the Protestant and Catholic perspectives in the next chapter, keeping in mind the diversity of thought on this subject within the Body of Christ.

Chapter 5

BAPTISM IN THE HOLY SPIRIT: PROTESTANT AND CATHOLIC PERSPECTIVE

The Church's history of attempting to reach a consensus on a variety of issues, thereby establishing and formalizing foundational orthodox doctrine, has yielded many resolutions over the centuries. Among these resolutions we find those pertaining to baptism in the Holy Spirit. Some of these resolutions came from councils, others from treatises. As we begin this chapter, we will very briefly note some of these resolutions from both the Protestant and Catholic perspectives, beginning in the fourth century.

Unity within the Body of Christ is important because ultimately unity brings strength, and strength is needed if we are to withstand the attacks of satan as we welcome the fruits of revival (new believers) until Christ returns for His victorious Bride. Therefore, I have included the Catholic perspective on baptism in the Holy Spirit in this book. I believe we should recognize Catholics as likely of receiving saving grace, just as we recognize Lutherans and Reformed, and the way to do this begins with an understanding of the history of the Catholic Church and those within it who have played a key role in the outpouring of the Spirit in the 20th Century, i.e., Roman

Catholic popes. We will examine the actions of several Catholic popes regarding baptism in the Holy Spirit, but first let us consider the impact of doctrine (on baptism in the Holy Spirit) that emerged from four councils in the fourth century. These four councils were convened in Europe, specifically in Spain, France, and Caesarea, which is part of modern-day Israel, and give evidence to the fact that baptism in the Holy Spirit was an important and integral part of the life of the fourth-century Church.

The Council of Elvira, also known as the Synod of Elvira, convened by the Church in Spain, was an attempt to restore discipline and order to the fourth-century Spanish Church. Like its counterpart, and the Council of Neocaesarea (A.D. 314), discussion included the importance of the bishop and his role in praying for those who have been baptized in order that they may be perfected, stressing the use of holy oil. Beginning in A.D. 353, the Church in France convened the Council of Arles to formally condemn the heresy of Donatism. Donatists were a Christian sect who refused to accept the spiritual authority of those in leadership in the Church who had fallen from grace during the persecution of Roman emperor Diocletian. Church leaders at the First and Second Council of Arles decided not to require these fallen leaders, and other Christians who had also denied their faith, to be re-baptized but instead to have them confirmed with the imposition of hands so that they would receive the Holy Ghost.[1] The General Council of Constantinople, A.D. 381, also expressed the need for anointing with oil as the "seal of the gift of the Holy Ghost."[2]

In addition to the work of these and many other councils, a body of written works emerged from the early Church. Among the more well known of these writings are the Apostolic Constitutions of the third and fourth centuries, which are now considered of great value to the Church historically. The *Apostolic Constitutions* come to us from the Ante-Nicene Fathers and are a collection of eight treatises that set forth the Church's authoritative recommendations regarding liturgy, Church organization, and the moral conduct of believers. Among other issues of the Church, they address the subject of baptism in the Holy Spirit:

> But thou shalt first anoint the person with the holy oil, and afterwards thou shalt baptize him with water, and in the conclusion thou seal him with ointment; that the anointing with oil may be the participation of the Holy Spirit, and the water the symbol of the death of Christ, and the ointment the seal of the covenants.[3]

The *Apostolic Constitutions* also provide the following instructions for the anointing to be filled with the Holy Spirit:

> Lord God, who art without generation, and without a superior. The Lord of the universe, who hast scattered the fragrance of the knowledge of the Gospel among all nations, do thou grant, at this time, that this ointment may be efficacious upon him that is baptized, so that the sweet odor of thy Christ may continue upon him firm and fixed, and that, having died with Him, he may rise with Him, and live with Him.
>
> Let him say these and the like things; for this is the efficacy of the laying of hands on each. For, unless there be such an invocation made by a pious priest over every one of these, the candidate for baptism only descendeth into the water, as do the Jews; and He putteth off only the filth of the body, not the filth of the soul.[4]

Additionally, the *Apostolic Constitutions* recommend that the following prayer be prayed by a bishop when he is ordaining a presbyter:

> I, who was beloved by the Lord, make this constitution for you the Bishops: When thou ordainest a Presbyter, Bishop, lay thy hand upon his head, in the presence of the Presbyters and Deacons, and pray, saying, Lord

Almighty, our God, who hast created all things by Christ, and dost in like manner take care of the universe by him; for he who had power to make different creatures, hath also power to take care of them, according to their different natures. On which account, God, thou takest care of immortal beings by preservation alone, but of those that are mortal, by succession; of the soul, by the provision of laws; of the body, by the supply of its wants. Do thou thyself, therefore, even now look upon thy holy church, and increase it, and multiply those that preside in it, and grant them power, that they may labor in word and deed for the edification of thy people. Do thou thyself also now look upon this thy servant, who is put into the Presbytery by the vote and determination of the whole clergy. *And do thou replenish him with the spirit of grace and counsel,* to assist and govern thy people with a pure heart, in the same manner in which thou didst look upon thy chosen people, and didst command Moses to choose elders, *whom thou didst fill with thy Spirit. And now, Lord, bestow and preserve in us the spirit of thy grace, that this person,* **being filled with the gifts of healing** *and the word of teaching,* may in meekness instruct thy people, and sincerely serve thee with a pure mind and a willing soul; and may fully discharge the holy ministrations for thy people, through thy Christ, with whom glory, honor, and worship, be to thee and to the Holy Spirit forever. Amen.[5]

This passage reveals that at this time, the Church expected those ordained as presbyters to be filled with the Holy Spirit at the time of their ordination through the bishop's laying on of his hands and his prayer. The prayer itself draws upon the example of Numbers 11:17, which records the Spirit that was on Moses being given to the 70 elders. When this happened, they all prophesied and received a spirit of wisdom (see Num. 11:25). As well, First Timothy 4:14 and Second Timothy 1:6 connect gifts given at ordination with the laying on of hands. This should not be considered the initial time the person was filled with the Holy Spirit, but another special occasion of being filled again, and especially with the gifts needed for the ministry into which he was being ordained.

The *Apostolic Constitutions* indicate that at least two rites emphasize a special work of baptizing or filling with the Spirit. The first occurred immediately after baptism as part of the conversion-initiation process. It entailed the laying on of the bishop's hands (or the priest's if the bishop was unable to be present) when the newly baptized person was anointed with oil for the second time. (The first anointing took place before entering the water for baptism, and the second occurred immediately following the baptism.) The bishop laid hands on the person, anointed him or her with oil, and then prayed the above prayer.

Clearly, the Protestant Church embraced the necessity and benefits of baptism in the Holy Spirit for all believers, even as they wrestled with various nuances of meaning concerning when and how this baptism was to occur. Just as the Protestant Church wrestled with issues surrounding baptism in the Holy Spirit, so did the Catholic Church. As we shall see, a number of Roman Catholic popes played a key role in the outpouring of the Spirit witnessed in the 20th century. Beginning in the late 1800s, Pope Leo XIII called for a Novena (nine days of prayer) to the Holy Spirit, asking that the entire Catholic Church participate in this prayer. On January 1, 1901, Pope Leo sang a song asking for a fresh outpouring of the Holy Spirit upon the whole Church. Years later, in 1967, it was this song being sung by the students at a retreat house at Duquesne University that birthed the Catholic Charismatic Renewal. It is of note that the Pentecostal movement also began in January 1901.

Fast-forward some 83 years, to 1984, when Pope John Paul II made the following request: "I ask you and all the members of the

Charismatic Renewal to continue to cry aloud to the world with me—'Open the doors to the Redeemer....'"[6] Then, in 1998, before a crowd of 300,000, he said, "Today, I would like to cry out to all of you gathered here in St. Peter's Square, and to all Christians: Open yourselves docilely to the gifts of the Spirit! Accept gratefully and obediently the charisms which the Spirit never ceases to bestow on us! Do not forget that every charism is given for the common good, that is, for the benefit of the whole Church."[7] Near the end of his life, Pope John Paul II is said to have remarked, "Thanks to the Charismatic movement, many Christians, men and women, youth and adults, have rediscovered Pentecost as a living and present reality in their daily lives. My desire is that the spirituality of Pentecost be spread in the Church."[8] As a result of these actions, and others, Charismatic renewal has continued in the Catholic Church, although it has been constrained in some instances.

The 21st-century Catholic Church has experienced a renewed interest in the work of the Holy Spirit through the efforts of Pope Benedict XVI, who has made many statements in support of the work of the Spirit in the life of the believer such as the following:

> I hope the Holy Spirit will meet with an ever more fruitful reception in the hearts of believers so that the "culture of Pentecost" will spread, so necessary in our time."[9]
>
> Let us rediscover, dear brothers and sisters, the beauty of being baptized in the Holy Spirit; let us be aware again of our baptism and of our confirmation, sources of grace that are always present.[10]
>
> Since 1967 over 120,000,000 Catholics in over 220 countries in the world have experienced this refreshment of the Holy Spirit. The promise Christ gave to His followers, the experience of Pentecost, the lineage of 2,000 years, the open window of Vatican II in the 1960s, are all a part of what the Catholic Charismatic Renewal is

today. Like all who have gone before, continue to pray, "Come, O Creator Blessed."[11]

Pope Benedict's successor, Pope Francis, has also advocated strongly for a renewed emphasis on the Holy Spirit. His June 2014 speech at the Charismatic Renewal Conference in Rome reflects this emphasis.

> You, Charismatic Renewal, have received a great gift from the Lord. You were born of the will of the Spirit as "a current of grace in the Church and for the Church." This is your definition: a current of grace....
>
> I have been asked to tell the Renewal what the Pope expects from you.
>
> The first thing is conversion to the love of Jesus, which changes life and makes of the Christian a witness of the Love of God. The Church expects this witness of Christian life and the Holy Spirit helps us to live the coherence of the Gospel for our holiness.
>
> I expect from you that you share with all, in the Church, the grace of Baptism in the Holy Spirit (expression that is read in the Acts of the Apostles).
>
> I expect from you an evangelization with the Word of God, which proclaims that Jesus is alive and loves all men.
>
> I expect that you give witness of spiritual ecumenism with all those brothers and sisters of other Churches and Christian communities who believe in Jesus as Lord and Savior.
>
> That you remain united in the love that the Lord Jesus asks of us for all men, and in the prayer to the Holy Spirit to come to this unity, necessary for evangelization in the name of Jesus.

Remember that "the Charismatic Renewal is by its very nature ecumenical. Catholic Renewal rejoices over what the Holy Spirit carries out in the other Churches" (1 Malines 5, 3).

Be close to the poor, the needy, to touch in their flesh the flesh of Jesus. Be close, please!

Seek unity in the Renewal, because unity comes from the Holy Spirit and is born of the unity of the Trinity. From whom does division come? From the devil! Division comes from the devil. Flee from internal fights, please! They must not exist among us!…

Brothers and sisters, remember: adore the Lord God: this is the foundation! To adore God. Seek sanctity in the new life of the Holy Spirit. Be dispensers of the grace of God. Avoid the danger of excessive organization.

Go out into the streets to evangelize, proclaiming the Gospel. Remember that the Church was born "in going forth" that Pentecost morning. Be close to the poor and touch in their flesh the wounded flesh of Jesus. Let yourselves be led by the Holy Spirit, with that freedom, and please, do not cage the Holy Spirit! With liberty!

Seek the unity of the Renewal, unity that comes from the Trinity! And I await you all, Charismatics of the world, to celebrate, together with the Pope, your Great Jubilee in Pentecost of 2017, in Saint Peter's Square! Thank you![12]

The Contemporary Catholic Church

Thus far, I have focused much of my discussion on the Roman Catholic Church's historical understanding of being baptized in or filled with the Holy Spirit, paying particular attention to the sacrament of initiation, which is baptism, and the laying on of hands, which later became known as confirmation. Baptism and confirmation have been, and are still, the experiences where, according to Catholic theology, there is the expectation that people will be filled with the Spirit.

A modern catechism of the Catholic Church states:

> He [the bishop] goes on to pray that those who receive the sacrament may be given "the fullness of royal, priestly, and prophetic power." With chrism the Christian is, so to speak, Christified.
>
> Confirmation exists to extend to the Church of every time and place the Gift of the Holy Spirit sent to the apostles on Pentecost. The Holy Spirit is the gift of Christ....
>
> Confirmation is thus the sacrament whereby the apostles and their successors, by the laying on of hands and anointing with chrism, communicate to the whole Church and all its members the gift of the Spirit received at Pentecost.[13]

Since 1967, when the Catholic Charismatic Renewal began at Duquesne University, a Catholic college in Pittsburgh, Pennsylvania, the Catholic Church has attempted to welcome this renewed grace of the Spirit and accommodate it to the liturgy and theology of baptism and confirmation. In particular, Cardinal Léon-Joseph Suenens, Father Raniero Cantalamessa, and Harold Cohen have advocated for an increased focus on the work of the Holy Spirit.[14] Cantalamessa sees the baptism in the Holy Spirit as a God-given means of freeing the grace of baptism when bound by a person's lack of faith. Cohen, for his part, gives a great illustration of how the current renewal of the Spirit works with the sacraments related to the baptism in the Holy Spirit:

Pentecost comes to each of us in the Sacraments of Initiation: Baptism, Confirmation, and Eucharist. In Baptism we receive the Holy Spirit and become God's children and members of the body of Christ. In Confirmation we receive a new fullness of the Spirit and are empowered to serve the Church and bear witness to Jesus.

Often we do not allow the Spirit we have received to be as active in us as He wants to be. To use an analogy, He is like chocolate syrup poured into a glass of milk—it goes to the bottom of the glass until stirred up. But when it is stirred up, it permeates the milk and transforms it into something new. We can learn how to "stir up" the Spirit—and how to receive more of Him—from Jesus in the Gospels.[15]

Chapter 6

Baptism in the Holy Spirit: The Holiness and Pentecostal Perspective

The historical significance of the baptism of the Spirit in the Ancient Church during the first 1,000 years, and our subsequent jump to the 20th century, is done so that one can see the evidence for the baptism and transference of gifts by the Holy Spirit. Although sometimes occurring through rituals and ceremonies, baptism has existed since the early Church, and the laying on of hands in prayer for the baptism of the Spirit continues to this day.

This division by the Catholic and Orthodox Churches of the experience of forgiveness from the experience of being filled with the Holy Spirit and having His gracelets (gifts) released in our lives that was seen in baptism and the laying on of hands (confirmation) would be seen again within Protestantism, particularly within the Anglican Church. John Wesley was the key Protestant leader who emphasized a distinction between the experience of justification and that of sanctification. Let us now look to him to gain an understanding of the basis of both the Holiness and Pentecostal teachings regarding a second definite work of grace, the experience of sanctification-baptism in the Holy Spirit, and the Pentecostal understanding of baptism in the Holy Spirit as a subsequent experience to salvation.

Arminian, Reformed, and Other Protestant Churches

Arminian, John Wesley 1703-1791

John Wesley was an Anglican who was used of God as a revivalist-evangelist. Later in life, he broke away from Anglicanism and founded the Methodist denomination. He did so because the Anglican Church would not send a bishop to ordain his ministers in America, due to the Revolutionary War. Wesley ordained two men, Coke and Asbury, as bishops. These actions resulted in a break with Anglicanism for the American churches under Wesley and his bishops Coke and Asbury.

Wesley was known to have people tremble, shake, and fall down during his meetings (later called "swooning" or being "slain in the Spirit").[1] This first happened to him at Fetter Lane in London shortly after his conversion at Aldersgate, which was so profound that it made him question if he was even saved prior to this experience at Aldergate,[2] even though he had graduated from Oxford, been ordained, and traveled to the colony of Georgia as a missionary. A record of Wesley's experience at Fetter Lane—which I believe was one of the events in his life when he experienced God's empowering presence—provides the following account:

> The new year was ushered in by a very extraordinary service held in the evening of New Year's Day, 1739. Messrs. Hall, Kinchin, Ingham, Whitefield, Hutchins, and the two brothers Wesley were present at a love-feast at Fetter Lane, with about sixty others, the number of the Fetter Lane Society at that time. "About three o'clock in the morning," Wesley says, "as we were continuing instant in prayer, the power of God came mightily upon

us, insomuch that many cried out for exceeding joy, and many fell to the ground. As soon as we were recovered a little from that awe and amazement at the presence of His Majesty, we broke out with one voice, 'We praise Thee, O God; we acknowledge Thee to be the Lord.'"[3]

Wesley taught that "miracles and spiritual giftings experienced in the early church were still present" in the 18th century, and I believe he would think miracles and giftings still exist today.[4] Like future Pentecostals, Wesley emphasized that a "second blessing" would occur in a moment as an experience with the Holy Spirit, one that carries its own sense of awareness.[5] Wesley's followers and future Pentecostals both reasoned that the fullness of salvation is participation in the divine life (sanctification)—more than simply the removal of guilt (justification). They believed this experience of the fullness of salvation with its corresponding full assurance of salvation was only possible after the second blessing or baptism of the Holy Spirit.[6] I believe that history will concur that just as the Lutherans were used of God to rediscover justification, the Anglican revivalists who became Methodists, and who were influenced by the Moravians, were similarly used of God to re-emphasize sanctification as a second work of the Holy Spirit within Protestantism. Wesley wrote that all of the testimonies he knew of regarding sanctification, which he later referred to as "baptism in the Spirit," were instantaneous instead of progressive and were self-evident.[7]

Wesley believed the expectation of being sanctified or baptized in the Holy Spirit was necessary for revival. He wrote, "Till you press the believers to expect *full salvation* now, you need not look for any revival."[8] "Full salvation" was another of his many terms for sanctification or baptism in Holy Spirit, as were "perfection" and "holiness."[9]

Wesley believed that one was justified by faith alone and that this justification did not depend upon feeling. However, he also believed that only when one was sanctified/baptized in the Holy

Spirit could one have full assurance of salvation. He believed that the only way for a Christian to have victory over sin was to be baptized in the Holy Spirit.[10] Apart from this, he reasoned, one could not be victorious or mature, a father rather than a babe in Christ. It was the Pentecostal work of the Spirit that gave believers victory over the flesh and dominion over sin.[11]

Wesley and John William Fletcher were influenced by the Church Fathers, which caused them to have a much stronger focus upon sanctification than Lutheranism emphasized. As a result, both Wesley and Fletcher were accused by the Calvinist Methodists of being guilty of embracing the Roman Catholic doctrine of good works and of thereby abandoning the Protestant doctrine of justification by faith.[12] The Calvinist Methodists, associated with George Whitefield, greatly outnumbered the Arminian Methodists associated with the Wesleys at that time (around 1770). Their accusations would prove false, for Wesley believed in a justifying faith and salvation by faith alone.

I believe there is great wisdom in rediscovering Wesley in such a time as this because he understood the dangers of unbalanced theology. He did not overemphasize Christology, with its focus being on justification through Christ by faith, nor did he overemphasize pneumatology, with its focus being on sanctification through the Holy Spirit. Rather, he sought to underscore both equally. He saw the danger of mysticism's emphasis on subjectivity, where our inner hearing of Rhema becomes more important than hearing from the Bible. He also saw the danger of placing emphasis on the Word to such an extent that sanctification was undermined. Wesley realized that overemphasizing the Spirit could lead one to undermined justification by faith. He believed both needed to be stressed.[13]

Fletcher and Wesley both believed that the highest level of grace was the Pentecostal grace experienced during the sanctification-baptism in the Holy Spirit. According to them, only during the baptism could a person be matured, becoming a father, instead of a young man or child. This experience granted the person full assurance of salvation and helped him or her avoid three traps of the enemy: pharisaic moralism, antinomian lawlessness, and monistic mysticism. In our time, I believe these threats exist, on the one hand, in Christian religious legalism and, on the other hand, in an overemphasis on justification or hyper-grace to the point that there is no accentuation of sanctification. Some of the hyper-grace messages teach that even to confess one's sins is seen as a failure to believe in grace. I would like to point out that grace has an aspect in justification, but there is also an aspect of grace as divine power that is associated with and necessary for sanctification. The mystical monism is present today in the New Age religions.

I believe God is doing, and has been doing, something within the Church that is very dear to His heart. He has been encouraging the ecumenical movement—encouraging Christian believers to love one another more and to leave divisions behind. I believe this desire of God's heart was a primary purpose for the Charismatic movement of the 1960s that caused Evangelicals, Episcopalians/Anglicans, Lutherans, Presbyterians, Baptists, Pentecostals, and Catholics to believe that God had truly saved for Himself people in all these denominations. This ecumenical movement is important if we are to partner with God in what He has prioritized for our time.

I understand now what Tommy Reed meant when he said to me, "Randy, you know that Pentecostals have a lot in common with the Catholic Church, sometimes more than with other Protestant denominations." At the time, Tommy was a Pentecostal pastor of a large Assemblies of God Church in Buffalo, New York. What is of note here is that Catholics never became cessationists. Catholic doctrine allows for the separation of the works of justifying grace from sanctifying grace in the sacrament of baptism and the laying on of hands, or confirmation. The Church Fathers spoke of the incompleteness of those who had been baptized without receiving the laying on of hands and its resultant empowering of the Holy Spirit. And, like the Catholics of the East, the Orthodox Church maintained an emphasis upon theosis, or becoming like God by His grace—a similar emphasis to that of Wesley and later to Pentecostalism.

Of interest also is that both Wesley and Fletcher understood the significance of Holy Communion—the Lord's Supper, or the Eucharist. They believed that by taking Holy Communion, one had the opportunity to receive the "most significant means of experiencing the full sanctifying grace of God."[14] Wesley's theology goes beyond grace that justifies. He embraces an order of salvation that begins with justification, then continues in sanctification-baptism in the Spirit, and ends with glorification. This order is reflected in the liturgy of the Anglican Church.[15]

Peter Cartwright

Peter Cartwright was a great Methodist leader of the 1800s who was touched in the Cane Ridge revival. He witnessed people jerking, rising up, dancing, running, falling under the power of God, etc. After 1800, these types of phenomena have accompanied major revivals.[16] Wesley's leaders in America, Bishops Coke and Asbury, underscored the importance—even the necessity—of this second work of grace having the greatest victory in the believers' lives.[17]

Charles G. Finney

Charles G. Finney was a great revivalist in America in the 1800s. Hours after his conversion, he experienced a powerful baptism in the Holy Spirit. He felt waves of electricity—a sensation that he termed "liquid love." He describes his conversion as follows: "All of my feelings seemed to rise and flow out, and the utterance of my heart was, 'I want to pour my whole soul out to God.' The rising of my soul was so great that I rushed into the room back of the front office, to pray."[18] He continues:

> But as I turned and was about to take a seat by the
> fire, I received a mighty baptism of the Holy Ghost.

Without any expectation of it, without ever having the thought in my mind that there was any such thing for me, without any recollection that I had ever heard the thing mentioned by any person in the world, the Holy Spirit descended upon me in a manner that seemed to go through me, body and soul. I could feel the impression, like a wave of electricity, going through and through me. Indeed it seemed to come in waves and waves of liquid love; for I could not express it in any other way. It seemed like the very breath of God. I can recollect distinctly that it seemed to fan me, like immense wings. No words can express the wonderful love that was shed abroad in my heart. I wept aloud with joy and love; and I do not know but I should say, I literally bellowed out the unutterable gushings of my heart. These waves came over me, and over me, and over me, one after the other, until I recollect I cried out, "I shall die if these waves continue to pass over me." I said, "Lord, I cannot bear any more; yet I had no fear of death."[19]

Reformed, George Whitefield

George Whitefield was a revivalist who began his ministry at age 21 after being influenced by John Wesley. Whitefield witnessed people collapsing and convulsing in the presence of the Spirit. Of note here is a comment by Thomas Kidd concerning the life of George Whitefield and the First Great Awakening:

I am increasingly convinced that much of the renewal led by Whitefield, Edwards, and others, grew out of a greater focus on and confidence in the work of the Holy Spirit. I [have argued] that what distinguished the evangelicals of the Great Awakening from earlier movements was their focus on the "new birth" and on the work of the Spirit in revival and conversion. The leaders of the

Great Awakening did not see these emphases as innovative, of course, but recoveries of biblical doctrine and practice.[20]

The Keswick Movment

During the period from 1875 to 1920, the Keswick movement came onto the scene. This was primarily a conservative and Evangelical movement with a Reformed presence, with a strong Holiness emphasis. It held the beliefs that a majority of Christians are living in defeat and that the secret to living the victorious Christian life is consecration followed by an experience of being filled with the Spirit. This movement attained prominence through annual conventions in Keswick, England, as well as through the literature written by its teachers and followers.

The Keswick movement was influenced by some Wesleyan holiness and perfection teachings. Wesley had often used the phrase "Christian perfection" to make the point that he was not talking about absolute sinless perfection. He pointed out that only believers could experience Christian perfection, which is different than God's unique, absolute perfection. This qualification hinged on his definition of sin as "a voluntary transgression of a known law."[21] He admitted that even the best believers could be guilty of involuntary transgression but could still be considered sinless.

Wesley came to an understanding that the complete sanctification as a second work of grace could occur instantaneously at a point in time subsequent to one's justification, even with God's gradual working both preceding and following it. That teaching was caught by Robert Pearsall Smith, who brought it to southern England and helped spread it through meetings and conferences that would in time influence Keswick thought and teaching.

Reverend T. D. Harford-Battersby, a well-educated canon in the Church of England, hungered for something deeper in his heart. In 1875, he attended Holiness conferences at Oxford and Brighton,

England, and came away with a changed heart. "We were taken out of ourselves; we were led step by step, after deep and close searching of heart, to such a consecration of ourselves to God, as in the ordinary times of a religious life, hardly seemed possible...to the enjoyment of a peace in trusting Christ for present and future sanctification which exceeded our utmost hopes."[22] Hartford-Battersby and Quaker pastor Robert Wilson, who was also mightily touched by God through the Holiness conferences, decided to call together Christians from all over England to share in their experience and held a conference shortly after, on June 29, 1875. About 800 people from all over the United Kingdom attended. That meeting led to yearly gatherings for the purpose of experiencing this second work of grace.

Some of the greatest names in the faith were associated with the Keswick movement: Hudson Taylor, Evan Hopkins, Andrew Murray, F. B. Meyer, and others. Holiness connected to the work of the Holy Spirit is not the domain of the Arminian or the Reformed or the Lutheran or the Catholic Church. It is a need for all theological or doctrinal positions. As already pointed out there is diversity in teachings about holiness and the experience of victory, but perhaps that is because there is diversity in the New Testament itself. Our need to systematize the Scripture into doctrinal systems causes us to build walls rather than bridges. The purpose of this book is to build bridges instead of walls to further the prayer of Jesus that we would all be one, or if that now seems too difficult an objective at this point in the history of the Church, that we would at least learn to love and honor each other as brothers and sisters in the family of God.

I believe the Bible does not fit either the Pentecostal or the Evangelical system regarding the baptism in the Holy Spirit; both are too narrow. I believe that the same God who did not make two fingerprints or two snowflakes alike did not intend to make our experience of His Spirit the same for everyone. When we look back at the passages in Acts, we find that the people were baptized in the Holy Spirit at a prayer meeting with tongues (see Acts 2) and at another prayer meeting without tongues (see Acts 4:31). Sometimes the Spirit came after baptism with the laying on of hands, with no tongues occurring (see Acts 8). At other times, we are not told the particulars of how or when someone was baptized with the Spirit (see Acts 9). Baptism in the Spirit can occur at the time of conversion, before water baptism, with tongues and prophecy accompanying it (see Acts 10). It can also occur after water baptism, with the laying on of hands, and can be accompanied by tongues and prophecy (see Acts 19). There appears to be at work here a God who likes diversity, and I suggest that we, too, need to learn to like diversity. I believe that if we could learn to appreciate this biblical variety, it would enable us to appreciate the differences within the Body of Christ, which satan has used to divide us.

In the Vineyard Church, a church in the St. Louis area that I pastored, we honored and welcomed people who had experiences reflecting this New Testament diversity. We did not try to convince them that their experiences were not valid or not normative. Rather, we emphasized that God was free to baptize us and fill us with His Spirit in whatever way He chooses. It is in this manner that we can find unity in the midst of diversity.

As a matter of fact, my emphasis has not been so much on the experience of being baptized in the Spirit as it has been on the fruit of having an intimate relationship with Jesus Christ. The reason I have encouraged the people of my church not to ask people if they have been baptized in the Spirit is that the answer does not really tell one much. What do I mean by this? Well, it is like asking someone if they have had a wedding: they may answer "yes," but that does not tell you anything about the relationship. They may be living in marital hell or matrimonial bliss. They may have had a wedding but are now divorced, widowed, or separated. One does not really know much about the relationship by asking someone if he or she has had a wedding. Instead, ask people about how intimate they are with their mate and if they love him/her more today than when they first married.

In like manner, people could have had an experience they call the baptism in the Holy Spirit years ago and could now either be cold, lukewarm, and/or backslidden or passionately in love with God. Focus on the relationship. In doing so, people cannot hide behind an experience of the past. It is not enough to have had a baptism in the Holy Spirit; we must continue to be filled with the Holy Spirit. Continuing this filling keeps us concerned about the full salvation of others, which includes healing and deliverance. For with the baptism of the Holy Spirit "comes a new revelation of the ache in God's heart for the saving of His children."[23]

Not only does the Bible record a diversity of experiences pertaining to the baptism of the Holy Spirit; the history of the Church does also. I must believe that Jesus was right when He made the reception of power the evidence of the Holy Spirit (see Luke 24:49 and Acts 1:8). When I read the history of the Church, I find men who had received power and then had a powerful influence upon the Church and society. Some of these people, like Francis of Assisi, Ignatius Loyola, Francis Xavier, and Mother Teresa (just to mention a few), were Roman Catholic; others, like George Whitefield and Billy Graham, were/are Reformed; others, like John Wesley, E. Stanley Jones, and Charles Finney, were Arminians; and still others, like Maria Woodworth-Etter, John G. Lake, Smith Wigglesworth, T. L. Osborn, Oral Roberts, Omar Cabrera, Carlos Annacondia, Claudio Freidzon, Luis Palau, and David Yonggi Cho, were/are Pentecostals. I cannot believe that the non-Pentecostals mentioned above were not baptized with the Holy Spirit simply because they did not speak in tongues and that others who have spoken in tongues but have had little impact upon the Church and society have been baptized in the Spirit. If power is a major purpose and evidence of the baptism in the Holy Spirit, then I must acknowledge that both Church history and the Bible indicate that people can have diverse experiences of the baptism in the Holy Spirit.[24]

Bible teacher and Christian author Don Basham, who became a leader in the Shepherding movement that originated in the 1970s, and editor of *New Wine* magazine, a monthly periodical published by Good News Church in Ft. Lauderdale, Florida, taught extensively on the Holy Spirit, among other things. The following is a quote from his *A Handbook on Holy Spirit Baptism* regarding the necessity of believers embracing baptism of the Spirit:

> Let us strive to be spiritual leaders of the Church, willing to pay the price of putting His Kingdom before our own. May we desire to have many repeated fillings of the Spirit in order that we might be known as men and women full of the Holy Spirit. Let us humble ourselves before God that He might lift us up. Let us truly acknowledge our personal weakness that we might turn from self and the flesh to Christ and the power of his Spirit. Let us love one another as mutual leaders in His Church and pray for each other, confess our sins to each other and carry each other's burdens. Let us quit fighting each other and fight the real enemy, satan, who accuses the brethren. Being baptized in the Holy Spirit is a way for us to glorify Jesus and reveals to us the depth of God's love.[25]

I appreciate the spirit of Bashan's words and pray that those of us living in the 21st century may see a mighty movement of God's Spirit that causes a great revival of power and an advance of the ecumenical Spirit that longs to fulfill Jesus' prayer of John 17 that we would become one as He and the Father are one. I believe we can become more united as we allow the Scripture to be the basis of this unity and allow for diversity that the Scripture contains.

Though I may not prefer the language some of the above people used to explain the experience of baptism in the Spirit, I am grateful for their openness to the experience itself, and their encouraging those within their expression of Church to embrace such an experience. I even appreciate their attempt to create language that allows those within their expression of Church, their denominational heritage, to experience the reality of the baptism while maintaining their denominational understanding of the relationship between justification-regeneration and sanctification and baptism in the Spirit.

PART TWO

EXPERIENCING THE BAPTISM OF THE HOLY SPIRIT

Dr. Randy Clark

Chapter 7

RECEIVING THE BAPTISM
IN THE HOLY SPIRIT

In the years since the revival began in Toronto in January 1994, I have been privileged by God's grace to meet key leaders of Catholic, Evangelical, and Pentecostal streams. What I discovered, and continue to discover, is that there is much more openness to a diversity of spiritual experiences than there was 20 years ago. I find Pentecostals and Catholics amenable to working with me, knowing that I do not believe one must speak in tongues to be baptized in the Spirit. Although I have had a prayer language since 1971, it did not occasion my baptism in the Holy Spirit. At the same time, I am finding Evangelicals who are open to working with me, even knowing that I do believe in the gifts of the Spirit and in the baptism of the Spirit as an experience that can occur both simultaneous with and, more often than not, following conversion. I am meeting Evangelical men and women who admit they were baptized in the Holy Spirit after their conversion, and I am meeting Pentecostals who acknowledge that they believe one could be baptized in the Holy Spirit before receiving one's prayer language, at the time one receives it, or after one receives it. I am discovering a growing favor among Roman Catholics, even though I don't hold to some of the doctrines or positions of Roman Catholicism. I consider it a great opportunity to meet with Catholics—professors, priests, and laypeople—who have a zeal for the Lord and who are familiar with the Holy Spirit working in their lives. It is the Holy Spirit who is bringing about a growing acceptance and love among the children of God. I call this reality "Holy Spirit ecumenism." He and the rest of the Trinity are the true basis for Christian unity.

I have given much thought to the requisite conditions, if there are any, for this spiritual experience of the baptism in the Holy Spirit. Three things stand out to me. First, it seems that the first possible condition is that we must become aware of our personal inadequacy in our Christian life— *"Very truly I tell you, no one can see the kingdom of God unless they are born again"* (John 3:3). We must recognize our defeated state, our indifference, our lack of power, our lack of faith, etc., if we are to understand and appreciate what it is Jesus is doing for us when He baptizes us with His Spirit.

Second, we must desire for our personal condition to change. By this I mean that we must develop a serious hunger to be victorious Christians. Jesus said, *"Blessed are those who hunger and thirst after righteousness"* (Matt. 5:6). God desires that our spiritual hunger be so great that we pant after that which He has to offer.

Third, we must want our lives to honor God and to be used in His service, for His glory. Second Peter 1:3-4 says, *"His divine power has given us everything we need for life and godliness through our knowledge of Him who called us by His own glory and goodness. Through these He has given us His very great and precious promises, so that through them you may participate in the divine nature and escape the corruption in the world caused by evil desires."* We are summoned by His energy to the glory of His name!

In light of these things, we are to seek and ask for power and gifts to make us commensurate to the tasks before us—binding the strong man and plundering his home as we break down the gates of hell. The experience of His presence and power is not a spiritual high for our own pleasure or gratification. His empowerment enables our faith to express itself in love. It is in our victory that God is glorified, honored, and pleased, and we are edified.

Evidences of Holy Spirit Baptism

There are often physical manifestations associated with the baptism of the Holy Spirit. These manifestations can create confusion because they are outside of our normal ways of functioning in the natural. It is important to understand that the Holy Spirit is sovereign. He will do what He chooses in His renewal of the human heart, even when it doesn't fit our paradigm.

One evidence of Holy Spirit baptism is shaking and trembling, which can be "mild or convulsive."[1] Trembling may occur in times of deliverance or healing or when one is under the power of the Holy Spirit. Another physical manifestation is joy that is often accompanied by singing or laughing, oftentimes causing people to burst into fits of euphoria. They may act "drunk" in the Holy Spirit, or cry or weep, especially in times of revival.[2] Furthermore, those overcome with the power of the Holy Spirit may dance or move around by jumping or leaping. They may also "fall out" in the Spirit, entering a trance-like state. Examples of this were seen in the First and Second Great Awakenings; the Cambuslang revival in Scotland; the Cane Ridge revival in Kentucky (which has been called "America's Pentecost"); Finney's revivals, where he described people falling out of their seats; the Holiness revival, the Pentecostal revival, the Latter Rain revival; the Charismatic revival; the Jesus movement; the Third Wave revival; the revival of the 1990s, sometimes called the "laughing revival"; and the Mozambique revival, led by Iris Ministries.[3]

In *An Essential Guide to Baptism in the Holy Spirit* we find the testimony of Pastor Ron Phillips of Abba's House in Hixson, Tennessee. He had typed his resignation letter on the plane ride to what he thought would be his last conference. While at that conference, Phillips heard the voice of God and felt His presence and anointing.

He writes in his book that he "wept, sang, laughed, shouted, shook, and lay at peace before [God]."[4] Following his baptism in the Holy Spirit, Phillips brought revival and awakening into his church.[5]

One of my spiritual sons, Paul Martini, received a fresh touch of the Spirit in 2014, accompanied by physical manifestations that indicated the strong presence of God. He describes the experience as follows:

> Heat that I had never felt before came over me like a vortex. I began to shake with what felt like electricity running through my body, while at the same time I would violently crunch my body as spasms of power hit me, all the while feeling tremendous heat. The spasms were so painful that with each one I felt as if I couldn't take it anymore. I was perspiring so heavily that I quickly soaked through my clothing. It was as if I had jumped in a pool of water. This experience continued for quite some time. I had no idea how long I was crouched in a ball on the floor. People around me said I was literally radiating heat.
>
> The fruit of these experiences has been dramatic. Up until this time I had not been experiencing a great deal of power when I ministered. I remember telling my wife and another friend that I knew God was using me for healing and teaching, but that I definitely didn't feel I had a commission for impartation. I knew there was fruit in my life, but not in the area of impartation. After that powerful experience with the Lord things began to change. I recall ministering to a crowd of several hundred. I was preaching when suddenly I felt like the Lord wanted me to stop and invite people to receive the fire of the Holy Spirit. I quickly closed the message and said, "If you want the fire of the Holy Spirit, come forward."

With that, about 500 people rushed to the front. I placed my hand on the first gentleman and he flew back three rows of chairs. After that, the meeting exploded. The fire of God fell on almost everyone there. I continued ministering until late into the evening. They moved us out of the room and I prayed for people for another two hours in the lobby. I had never seen so many people touched before through my hands.

Since then I have seen the revival fire of the Holy Spirit poured out on many people. God didn't just release to me an experience. He commissioned me to impart gifts to the Body of Christ. I have seen tremendous growth in myself as a result of God's touch. I am able to hear the Lord and follow where He is leading in a meeting. My preaching and teaching have become more effective. Most of all, I feel like a tool sharpened and upgraded for a greater capacity of the anointing of the Holy Spirit. The fruit continues to grow in significant ways. I have seen deaf ears open up, people on life support with no hope come back to life, cancerous brain tumors disappear, and even the crippled start to walk. All of this brings more glory to Jesus Christ. I'm so grateful for all that God has done and continues to do.[6]

Here is another modern-day example from Robert Martin, a pastor in the Christian and Missionary Alliance:

I am a pastor in the Christian and Missionary Alliance and have a Ph.D. in New Testament Studies from Southwestern Baptist Theological Seminary. I mention the Ph.D. simply to emphasize that the experiences, which are recounted below, and other of my experiences of the last two years have been carefully thought through biblically, theologically, and historically. The work of the Holy Spirit in my life has been a developing, progressive experience with several specific crisis points. Dr. Gordon Fee, the respected Pentecostal New Testament scholar, has written a book entitled *God's Empowering Presence: The Holy Spirit in the Letters of Paul.* In speaking of the debate over whether there is an experience subsequent to conversion called "baptism in the Holy Spirit," Dr. Fee writes, "Perhaps too much is made on both sides of single experiences. For Paul, life in the Spirit begins at conversion; at the same time that experience is both dynamic and renewable."[7] Keeping the fact in mind that the work of the Holy Spirit in our lives is a continuing and dynamic process, let me briefly relate three significant experiences that I have had. Rather than trying to distinguish any one as my "baptism in the Holy Spirit" or my being "filled with the Spirit," I see each of them as examples of the continuing work of the Holy Spirit in my life.

In April of 1994, I went to Arlington, Texas, to attend a conference on the Holy Spirit. Just preceding this conference was a meeting of Vineyard pastors in Plano, Texas, which a friend and I also attended. Several of these pastors had recently been to the Toronto Airport Vineyard and had been touched by the Holy Spirit there.

I come out of a very traditional Evangelical background and had never seen anything like the falling, laughing, and shaking that I saw in these meetings. I quickly sensed, however, that God was somehow in this. I heard of lives drastically changed and I saw peace and joy in these people. Even though I was somewhat apprehensive, I finally went forward for prayer. As I was walking forward, I told the Lord that I hoped I was not being hard-hearted but that if I fell down, it would have to be He that did it. As these Vineyard leaders began to pray for me, they prayed very quietly and they certainly were not trying to push me over because they did not even touch me. Suddenly, I felt a heat rising up my legs and I had to struggle just to stand up. I began to stumble around like a drunken man. The next thing I knew, I was lying on the floor. There was no great emotion as I lay there, but I had a great sense of peace. I also realized that my life would never be the same! In the next couple of days there was more prayer and I cried tears of repentance and brokenness. As I returned home, I could tell that something had happened and I knew that the Holy Spirit had touched me. As I prayed for people in my own church God began to touch them in a new way, too.

In June of 1994, my family and I went to some meetings in Fort Wayne, Indiana, where Randy Clark was speaking. I took my wife and two children, and God also powerfully touched them. (I am writing this almost two years later and their lives have never been the same.) We got acquainted with Randy Clark in Fort Wayne and in the next several months attended several of his meetings in different places.

In November of 1994, we attended a series of meetings in Greensboro, North Carolina. It was a Monday night meeting and we were still there at about two o'clock in the morning. Only a few people remained. We prayed for the pastor of the Vineyard, Lee O'Hare, and he was powerfully touched by God and began to shake. My wife, Debbie, turned to me and said, "Let us pray for you." I had had almost no physical manifestations in the months since God started this new work in me. I think that she hoped something might happen to me so I would have a better understanding of those who did have these manifestations. It was so late and I was so tired that I just lay down on the carpet and told them to pray for me. As I lay there, my feet began to tingle and the thought came to me that someone should grasp my feet and pray for me. All of a sudden I felt someone grab my feet, and I heard Randy Clark begin to pray. Then Randy moved up to my head and Lee went to my feet, and they began to pray. My wife was on one side of me and a friend named Greg was on my other side. They were all praying for me. All of a sudden something hit me, and I began to shake violently. Randy later said I looked like a frog being electrocuted. At the very moment that this power hit me, my wife and my friend Greg were knocked over backwards and began to laugh. After about 20 seconds the shaking stopped.

I had heard stories of people like D. L. Moody who had been powerfully touched by the Holy Spirit and had told the Lord to stay His hand because the experience was too intense. I had thought that if anything like that ever happened to me I would just say, "Enlarge the vessel" and I would tell the Lord to keep pouring it on. After 20 seconds of this experience, I couldn't take any more. In fact, Randy started to pray for the Lord to send another wave, and I started saying, "No, no, no." Sometime later, I got up and I felt physically sick (somewhat like Daniel did in Daniel 8:27 when he said he lay ill for several days after his encounter with the angel). I walked about 100 feet and was so weak and so overwhelmed that I just lay down on the floor. I believe that this whole experience was God giving me a little glimpse of how awesome and powerful He really is.

The final experience I will mention was when Randy Clark was in Wilmore, Kentucky, for a series of meetings. Jim Goll from Kansas City was speaking one morning.

He was speaking about Peter walking on the water and how Peter brought Jesus back to those in the boat who were afraid to step out. I sensed a calling from God to help people come into a deeper experience of Christ. As I sat there, I began to weep. I do not cry like this very often, and when I do, it does not last long. This time I just kept crying. They opened up the altar for people to come and pray, and I went up and lay there and sobbed for more than two hours. Randy later commented to me that he had never seen me so emotional. God had touched something very deep in me. It seems the Lord was clarifying His call on my life and was breaking and humbling me to prepare me for what He had for me.

I could recount many more evidences of the Holy Spirit's work in my life over the last two years, but I will stop here. These three experiences show that the Holy Spirit's work in our lives is a continuing one and will be expressed in the lives of different people in different ways. It may also be expressed in the same person in very different ways over the course of time. I want to close with the reminder that the greatest work of the Holy Spirit in our lives is to conform our characters to the image of Christ. The great aim of the Holy Spirit working in us is that we might be holy and that we might show forth in our lives in the purity, passion, and power of our Lord.[8]

Receiving the Baptism of the Holy Spirit

How does one go about receiving the baptism of the Holy Spirit? As we examine three different denominational approaches, you will see that there are more similarities than differences.

Evangelical

World-renowned evangelist Billy Graham has this to say about the power of the Holy Spirit in the lives of believers: "I think it is a waste of time for us Christians to look for power we do not intend to use: for might in prayer, unless we pray; for strength to testify, without witnessing; for power unto holiness, without attempting to live a holy life; for grace to suffer, unless we take up the cross; for power in service, unless we serve. Someone has said, 'God gives dying grace only to the dying.'"[9] I agree with Graham. We must be a people given over to God, eager to receive the empowering of His Spirit in our lives and our ministries.

Evangelist R. A. Torrey points out that there are seven steps that can be used to obtain the baptism in the Holy Spirit:[10]

1. The first step involves repenting and accepting Jesus as Christ and Lord.

2. The second includes changing one's mind about sin, renouncing it, and finding a place of honesty in one's heart.

3. The third step involves humbling ourselves in our confession of sin.

4. The fourth step is obedience and a "total surrender to the will of God."[11]

5. The fifth step, found in Luke 11:13, is having an intense desire in your heart to be baptized in the Holy Spirit.

6. The sixth step, also from Luke 11:13, is to ask for a blessing and baptism. Torrey believed that "what was given to the Church must be appropriated by each believer for himself."[12]

7. The seventh and final step is laid out in Mark 11:24 and states that one must have faith in order to receive the baptism.

These are all crucial steps in preparing oneself for receiving the baptism in the Holy Spirit. Imagine what the Church would look like if every believer fully embraced these seven steps in his or her life!

A. W. Tozer, the well-educated Dutch Reformed pastor, in his book *How to Be Filled with the Holy Spirit,* explains how to obtain the baptism, mentioning something that Torrey does not—that God's plan for you most certainly involves a baptism. Tozer states that the baptism is "part and parcel of the total plan of God for His people."[13] Similar to Torrey, Tozer also highlights the *desire* to be filled as a key element. Both men also discuss that to be filled, you must *belong* to God. You must be a believer who has given his or her life to Christ.

Another Evangelical, Don Basham, also weighs in on how to be filled with the Spirit in his book *A Handbook on Holy Spirit Baptism,* providing four steps to follow:

1. Find a place for quiet prayer.

2. Re-read the Scriptures where the Holy Spirit is promised.

3. Say a prayer of invitation to be filled. (This is similar to Torrey's and Tozer's belief that one must belong to God and be ready to receive.)

4. Once the Holy Spirit is received, one will speak the language of the Holy Spirit.[14]

5. One must continue walking in faith.[15]

Finally, the Baptist pastor A. J. Gordon, in *The Ministry of the Spirit,* notes that it is a privilege of believers to receive the Holy Spirit baptism. He believes that it is a conscious act of appropriating one's faith, just like when one receives Jesus Christ as his or her Savior.[16] Gordon goes on to say that believers are baptized with water, but this is not enough—the baptism of the Spirit itself must be appropriated. He recommends praying, "O Holy Spirit, I yield to thee now in humble surrender. I receive thee as my Teacher, my Comforter, my Sanctifier, and my Guide."[17] Gordon believes we must consciously accept Jesus as our Savior and the Holy Spirit as our Sanctifier in order to fully appropriate the baptism.

Pentecostal

To most modern Pentecostals, the baptism in the Holy Spirit as evidenced by tongues remains the sign of what it means to be Pentecostal.[18] Some early Pentecostal groups, including the Elim Alliance, a denomination in Britain, and the Pentecostal Assemblies of Canada, did not adhere to the strict view that the gift of tongues must accompany the baptism.[19] However, many Pentecostals still regard this gift as of paramount importance because it provides tangible evidence that one has received the power of the Holy Spirit. Furthermore, Pentecostals traditionally maintain the position that the filling with or baptism in the Holy Spirit is always subsequent to conversion. Taken together, these two beliefs—tongues as the necessary evidence of the baptism in the Spirit and the baptism's subsequence to conversion—form the pillars of Pentecostalism. But, as I've argued in this book, these guidelines are softening among many Pentecostal scholars today.

Catholic

According to Catholic doctrine, to prepare for the baptism of the Holy Spirit, "inner healing is often needed."[20] It is also important to preach on "God's personal, unconditional, tender love for each person."[21] Moreover, preparation for baptism includes equipping believers with "practical instruction on how to resist the tactics of the evil one."[22] Teachings are crucial that explain Jesus's forgiveness of sin and saving from sickness as well as how to receive and exercise the charisms of the Spirit.[23] Each person is sent forth by the Spirit, and "all Catholics are called to evangelize."[24] In Catholicism, Christians were expected to accept the faith and be confirmed as such.

Then, confirmed Christians were expected to receive the gifts of the Holy Spirit, which signifies an inauguration into the Church.[25]

The writings of St. Augustine of Hippo bring us theology that became foundational to both Catholicism and Protestantism. Regarding baptism of the Holy Spirit, Augustine wrote:

> "This intervention of the holy Spirit is not a sacrament. It is over and above the baptism with water and any other sacramental action of the Church. So it was with the apostles and the disciples who had been baptized with water, as Augustine is convinced, before the ascension of our Lord. So it was and still is for all the Christians who are baptized with the Spirit. "We must not think that those who have received a valid baptism have also automatically (*continua*) received the holy Spirit.'" The Pentecostal outpouring of the holy Spirit can be received only by those who, like the first believers, through prayer and spiritual longing have previously become new wineskins in order to receive the new wine*.
>
> When that preparation has been carried out, the outpouring of the Pentecostal Spirit may be prayed for. At this point it is very useful to note some doctrinal points that according to Augustine must be borne in mind when we pray for a renewed outpouring of the holy Spirit.[26]

Traditional walls are beginning to fall. Why? Because people are no longer satisfied with a tidy, supposedly theologically correct understanding of the baptism in the Holy Spirit. Desperation has risen in the hearts of people to experience what the Bible speaks of in such experiential terms. Millions of Christians have entered into their Pentecostal type of experience on all continents and among most denominations.

While I was attending seminary, I was told by Dr. Lewis Drummond about the great Shantung revival among the North China

Mission of the Southern Baptist Convention. Although I graduated in 1977, I had never read anything about the Shantung revival until I read the book, which I then reprinted in 1995, 18 years later. In the spring of 1994, for several weeks I felt recurring impulses to locate everything written about the Shantung revival and read it. I was captivated by this revival that occurred among Southern Baptist missionaries in 1932. It is clear that it began among the leadership, who were tired and burned out. They admitted their need for more and discovered that some of the leaders among them were not even truly born again. The emphasis of the Shantung revival was a study of the Bible relating to the Holy Spirit and a baptism of the Holy Spirit, and making sure one has been truly born again. As I read *The Shantung Revival*, I found everything that had been happening in the Toronto Blessing (except the animal sounds, which have been blown out of proportion). I write this now in 2016, and to the best of my knowledge, there have been only twelve times that there were animal sounds at the Toronto Airport Christian Fellowship, three of which happened in meetings I was leading. Considering there have been meetings six nights a week since January 20, 1994, in Toronto—for twelve-and-a-half years—and I have been in over 2,800 revival meetings, twelve occurrences is not indicative that this is one of the main things God has been doing in this revival.[27]

The other things that often occur in revival—the shaking, the falling, the crying, the laughing—all occurred in the Shantung revival. In fact, these things seem to happen everywhere people have been seeking the fullness of the Holy Spirit. I have found evidence of this in Protestant revivals from all over the world, in Roman Catholic histories of moves of God, and in the Bible. We are a people desperate for God and His empowerment unto salvation.

Chapter 8

IT IS THE SPIRIT WHO TESTIFIES

In the Book of Genesis and in the latter part of the Book of Job, we find the unfathomable creativity of God laid before us. In Genesis 1:2 we glimpse a picture of the mighty Spirit of God hovering over all of creation. The earth is formless, dark, and void of anything until the Spirit of God begins to hover over the waters and God pronounces light over the darkness. Suddenly, chaos begins to give way to order, and even light and darkness are given purpose and function in God's magnificent creation. This mighty work of the Spirit in creation continues today in us, and His creativity is no less unfathomable. I am constantly delighted and amazed at the ways in which God's Spirit touches us.

My friend Bill Johnson, a pastor and apostolic leader, shared the story of some of his relatives from his grandparents' generation who experienced a baptism of the Holy Spirit through the ministry of Smith Wigglesworth that bore itself out in the most beautiful manner. When the Spirit of God touched them, they took up pen and paper and began to write in an unknown language, which later proved to be Chinese. When these writings were translated, it was revealed that they were praises to God. Johnson's family still has those original writings. These experiences, and those of many others, cannot be categorized, leading me to ask, "Why should the ways in which we manifest the baptism of the Holy Spirit be any less creative than the One who gives us His Spirit?"

The divine dance of the Trinity, the beautiful perichoresis, leads us to the very nature of God, which in turn leads us to the nature He designed for us, for we are made in the image and likeness of God. The intimacy of the divine relationship is meant to be ours as well (see John 17:21). The term *perichoresis* is derived from the Greek *peri* and *chorein*—*peri* meaning "around" and *chorein* meaning "to make room for" or "contain." The Old Covenant temple served as a repository for God's presence. We are the New Covenant temple, built to host God's presence in the power of His Spirit if we will but "make room" for Him around us and in us.

One of my spiritual sons, Will Hart, who is an associate evangelist at Global Awakening, found himself making room for the Spirit one night on the floor in the basement of a small church in Massachusetts. Will was a rebellious young man, dabbling in satanism and drugs. You might say Will was formless and void in the midst of great darkness, when God's Spirit touched him that October night in 1999. He recounts the following encounter with the Holy Spirit:

> For me, salvation, deliverance, surrender, baptism, and impartation all took place in a 20-minute span on the floor of a small Assemblies of God church. It was what I will call a "full Sozo moment." One minute I was listening to the message and the next I started weeping. The speaker was a man named Bob who would become instrumental in my spiritual growth. I had heard the words "Jesus loves you" countless times before, but when Bob spoke them that night, the power of God backed them up. The precious embrace of God's love fell over my entire body, and I was completely undone by a baptism of love. There was no other response but

to run to the front of the room and cry out for more. When I did, I fell to the floor and lay there shaking violently. In between sobs I found myself crying out to God, saying, "I don't know what this is, but I want it."

Typical of Bob, he didn't leave me lying on the floor for long. In the midst of this incredible baptism of love, I felt the toe of Bob's shoe in my rib cage. "What are you doing on the ground, boy?" boomed Bob's voice. "It's time to go to work!" With that, Bob picked me up off the floor and stood me in front of a man waiting to receive prayer. I had never prayed for anyone like this before. Bob took my hands and placed them on the face of the man, and we both (not Bob, but the gentleman I was praying for) fell to the ground weeping. Bob's command, married with the touch of God, launched me into ministry that continues to this day. As I touched this man's face, I learned something from the Holy Spirit that many spend years trying to figure out: God had touched me for a reason. I was receiving His power for a purpose, and that purpose was to join with Him, to take up the cross and join Him in doing the work of the One who sent us Jesus.

It was as if God's Spirit had flipped some kind of hunger switch in me that night on the floor in Massachusetts. Up to that point I hadn't been hungry for much of anything. But after God touched me, I couldn't get enough of Him. I set my sights on being as close as possible to people who moved in the power of God. I would pour over videos and books by the hour. Someone gave me a biography of the life of William Branham, which I read for nine hours straight, weeping the whole time, crying out, "God, will You use me in the same way You used Branham?"

The fruit and fire of this initial encounter have not waned in my life. Quite the contrary, the fire continues to grow within me as I travel the world, speaking at events both large and small. It doesn't matter if it's a group of five people or five thousand—God always shows up with His power and His love to change lives. I have seen hardened child soldiers who have never heard the name of Jesus Christ drop their weapons and fall to their knees as I present the Gospel. I have seen young and old alike receive His touch. Children are especially receptive to God's Spirit, and I love introducing them to the great love of their heavenly Father.

I don't care where God sends me or to whom He sends me. All I know is that when you position your heart to be available to sow into others, God will meet you there. Whether it's two people or two thousand, when God provides the opportunity, go with excellence and give away everything you have, all of your heart. Don't hold back. The choice is yours. God will anoint you with power, but it is still up to you to put one foot in front of the other and "go." Your initial Holy Spirit baptism encounter with God is a milestone, but it is not the end; it is the beginning. He wants you to take what you have received and give it away. Like the boy with the loaves and fishes, take whatever is in your hand and give it to Jesus. Don't hold anything back. Jesus will take what you give Him, and while giving thanks, He will take you and break you. He will break what is common in your life and then He will shower you with the Holy Spirit and power. He wants to take your simple bread and fish and feed the multitudes. *"The harvest is plentiful, but the laborers are few. Ask the Lord of the harvest, therefore, to send out workers into His harvest field"* (Luke 10:2).[1]

The work of the Holy Spirit in our lives is a continuing, dynamic process—*"Now the Lord is the Spirit, and where the Spirit of the Lord is, there is freedom. And we, who with unveiled faces all reflect the Lord's glory, are being transformed into His likeness, with ever-increasing glory, which comes from the Lord, who is the Spirit"* (2 Cor. 3:17-18). Not only did Paul speak about glory, both God's glory and our participation in that glory, Jesus did so as well.

In the great Gospel of John, the beloved disciple tells us the powerful words of Jesus, *"But when He, the Spirit of truth, comes, He will guide you into all the truth; for He will not speak on His own initiative, but whatever He hears, He will speak; and He will disclose to you what is to come. He will glorify Me, for He will take of Mine and will disclose it to you"* (John 16:13-14 NASB). Then, later John goes on to say, *"This is the One who came by water and blood, Jesus Christ; not with the water only, but with the water and with the blood. It is the Spirit who testified, because the Spirit is the truth"* (1 John 5:6 NASB). God earnestly desires that we receive His Spirit of truth. Jesus tells His disciples that He must go away in order that they receive this precious Holy Spirit; that if they wait, they will receive what the Father has promised (see Luke 24:49). We no longer have to wait for the precious Holy Spirit. Jesus lives and sits at the right hand of the Father, and the Spirit is available to us for the asking. *"Ask and you will receive, and your joy will be complete,"* says Jesus (John 16:24).

The following account from Steve Stewart, pastor of Cambridge Vineyard in Ontario, Canada, gives witness to the fruit of Holy Spirit baptism:

> On Monday, January 24, 1994, in response to an invitation by John Arnott, I attended one of the meetings [in Toronto] led by Randy Clark. Although I saw a number of people obviously impacted by the Holy Spirit (i.e., laughing, crying, falling, shaking, etc.), I felt very much like an observer throughout the evening and did not go forward to receive prayer myself. A week later,

John Arnott again urged me to come attend another one of the meetings, and so on Tuesday, February 1st, I did so, accompanied by all of our pastoral staff. During the worship, three of my children went up to the front to be with John and Carol Arnott, and the Spirit of God fell upon the two youngest. John and Carol beckoned my wife and me to the front, where we found two of our children on the floor laughing and seemingly unable to get up, while another of my sons prayed over both of them. A few minutes later, Randy invited all of the pastors and their wives to receive prayer in an adjoining meeting room. My wife and I gathered along with our staff and approximately fifty other people. When I was prayed for, I felt the presence of the Lord come and rest upon me, albeit somewhat gently, and I rather quietly slumped to the ground. A few minutes later, I got up and, to my surprise, discovered almost all of our staff stretched out on the floor. As I stood there looking at them, John Arnott came over and, aware that he had a very sore throat, I offered to pray for him. Almost as soon as I laid my hands on him and began to pray, the power of God hit both of us and we both fell almost violently to the ground. Observers later said we looked like two bowling pins flying through the air. As soon as I hit the ground, the power of God fell upon me in a way I have never known before, and I began to laugh loudly and uncontrollably. This continued for several minutes, and then I found myself beginning to weep and feel extremely powerful muscle contractions around my middle. Frankly, it felt like what I imagine birth pains to be. For the next couple of hours I laughed and cried. I was also aware that I was having a great deal of trouble speaking. I stammered almost uncontrollably, and often I would "lock up" on a single word. I also began to fall over again and again. Almost invariably, once I felt that I was under control and could get up and walk, as soon as I tried to take some steps I would fall over again. This probably happened somewhere between 12 and 20 times. After some time, I began to pray for other pastors and leaders, and the power of God fell on many of them. Around one o'clock in the morning, some of the staff helped me out of the building and into our van. Needless to say, someone else drove!

This began what has been a most remarkable journey for me. Over the past six weeks, the power of God has not only fallen on me again and again, often without any warning whatsoever and often not even in the context of any meeting, but as well, I have prayed for hundreds and hundreds of people and have seen the Holy Spirit fall upon a very high percentage of them. I have just returned from Russia where, without me telling them anything about what has been going on in our own church, when I prayed for people, manifestations took place identical to those which took place here. People in Russia fell over, shook, laughed, and cried. There has been a significant amount of demonic manifestation as well. An interesting aspect of this, though, is that the demonic spirits leave almost immediately upon being addressed. We have been holding meetings for many weeks now in the Cambridge Vineyard and have seen countless hundreds touched by God.

John 15:26 and First John 5:7 both state that the Holy Spirit testifies to Jesus Christ. I would say that one of the most significant results of this move of God has been that we have experienced the common testimony of many that the presence and person of Jesus Christ have become so much more real. We certainly have seen more people come to Christ in the last six weeks than at any other six-week period in our history. This renewal has touched our small groups, children's ministry, junior-high teens and young adults' ministry. As a church, we find ourselves crying out simultaneously, "Thank You, Lord" and "Give us more, God, for we are not satisfied."

I hope the testimonies in this chapter have helped to create more faith and a greater hunger for the baptism in the Holy Spirit in your life. I have been blessed to watch Steve's transformed life since he was touched in Toronto in 1994. We have remained friends and have worked together on humanitarian projects.

Join me now as we move into Part Three of this book, written by Dr. Jon Ruthven. Jon was my mentor while I pursued a doctor of ministry degree at the United Theological Seminary. I have been greatly influenced by his insights into the theology of the Bible, especially in regard to the baptism in the Holy Spirit. What Jon writes goes well beyond my own former insights regarding the baptism, taking us from traditional views of the biblical basis for the baptism in the Spirit to a radical (in the sense of "returning to the root") understanding of it. After all, the baptism in the Spirit was the central mission—the explicit agenda—of Jesus when He was introduced in all four Gospels: "He will baptize you in the Holy Spirit" (see Matt. 3:11-12; Mark 1:7-8; Luke 3:16; John 1:32-33).

PART THREE

A NEW BIBLICAL UNDERSTANDING OF THE BAPTISM OF THE SPIRIT

Dr. Jon Ruthven

Amen!

Chapter 9

THE CENTRAL MISSION AND MESSAGE OF JESUS

I'm going to propose a shocking but, I believe, absolutely biblical proposal: the baptism of the Holy Spirit is not simply an "add-on" or secondary experience after "salvation" but was always the central goal of the Bible for all believers, even in this age; the baptism of the Holy Spirit was the primary mission of Jesus for His disciples, including us. "Wait!" you exclaim, "That's heresy! The central purpose of Jesus's coming was to die on the cross for our sins for our salvation!" I'll get to that. But first...

Theological Traditions on the Baptism in the Holy Spirit

A favorite theologian of mine once quipped: "There are three things you never want to see get made: laws, sausages, and theology!" He joked that "if you laid all of the theologians in the world end to end, they'd never reach a conclusion." If you don't believe me, just skim through the theology journals at any local seminary library and see for yourself. You will likely be amazed at how incurious theologians are about the explicitly stated mission and message of Jesus Himself: to baptize in the Holy Spirit.

As Randy mentioned in Part One, the Spirit-focused writings of Macchia, Fee, Deere, Suenens, and other, more recent scholars like Menzies, Max Turner, Wolfgang Vondey, Mark Cartledge, Veli-Matti Kärkkäinen, Graham Twelftree, Simon Chan, Michael Brown, and Amos Yong are the exception in academia, or even theology for that matter.

For example, one serious study of the most used seminary library reference books showed that whereas in the Gospel of Mark, a whopping 65 percent of words describing Jesus's public ministry were about acts of power, only 33 hundredths of one percent (0.33%) of the material in the most prominent reference books was about the same topic: healings, miracles, or signs and wonders![1] Why bring this up here? Because these acts of God's power are essentially acts of the Holy Spirit. These are revelations in "deed" just as prophecy is revelation in "word." Note that Jesus and Paul were mighty in "deed and word" as they expressed their "Gospel" as a result of Spirit-baptism and modeled it for others (see Luke 24:19; Rom. 15:18).

Traditional theology, however, has denied or distorted the work of the Spirit today. The founders of the Protestant movement, Luther and Calvin, denied that spiritual gifts continued to be given after the close of the canon only because their opponents, the Roman Catholics, were appealing to these spiritual gifts to prove the validity of their doctrinal positions.[2] In the New Testament, however, the revelation of God in miracles doesn't "prove" the Gospel—it expresses the Gospel.[3] Because of this cessationist stance, the Reformers had no place to take their theology beyond their version of the Catholic Mass, which had become the center of Christian life. The Reformers did not "reform" that much; they just cleaned up some abuses while maintaining the traditional theological structure—after all, they were raised as Catholics.

In practice, the Christian was to be a consumer of religious services and information. The attitude was "Jesus paid for our sins; now our job is to act out our salvation by being good, going to church, and going to Heaven." A century later, 1647 to be exact, the Westminster Confession of Faith, what has been termed the "gold standard" of Protestant theology, insisted that God's revelation was now "wholly" reduced to Scripture because "those former ways of revelation [miracles and prophecy] had ceased." As a result, generations of Protestant scholars were limited in their theology, arguing endlessly over "salvation" and its various, elaborate stages. They saw the Holy Spirit's work as limited to foreknowledge, predestination, calling, regeneration, faith, repentance, justification, adoption, perseverance, mortification, sanctification, and glorification. The Bible, then, served only as a source of "proof texts" to support their pre-existing positions on "salvation." The Protestant "Gospel" consisted of a verbal or written creed, which, when illuminated and activated by the Spirit, would result in "salvation."

Now, ultimately there is nothing more important in our universe than avoiding hell, which is a very real horror and far beyond catastrophic, and attaining Heaven. The problem is, traditional theology has minimized *"the power of God unto salvation,"* that is, the biblical emphasis on how to get there—the "seal of the Spirit," the presentation and outworking of the Gospel using all the protecting tools of the New Covenant spiritual gifts (Rom. 1:16 KJV). Like a seal on a scroll, the pages cannot be accessed until the seal is broken. Likewise, when one is "sealed by the Spirit" on the way to being "delivered" into the heavenly court, that person can be accessed only by God Himself. The Spirit's "seal" is manifested as spiritual gifts, protecting us on our journey to Heaven with prophecy, words of wisdom, healing, miracles, etc.

Not only does Protestant theology not emphasize the gifts of the Spirit as the New Testament means for promoting salvation; it actually denies them. It redefines the baptism as a much less visible working of the Spirit that is often more assumed than shown to be real. The traditional Protestant system has no room for the explicit, stated mission of Jesus—the baptism of the Holy Spirit.

To Protestants, if such a thing happened at all, it happened mostly invisibly—*ex opere operato*, meaning it happened because ritual says so—within one of the stages of salvation, the *ordo salutis*. Certainly, there could be no expression of spiritual gifts—tongues, prophecy, healing, etc.—because such manifestations could be used only to introduce new doctrine or prove sainthood (apostleship), neither of which occur after the New Testament period. If such gifts did seem to appear, they were dismissed as counterfeit—"lying wonders" to confirm the doctrines of the Catholics or the antichrist, which to Protestants back then was pretty much the same thing.

In this, the Reformers utterly missed the "big picture" of Jesus's purpose with His disciples: to empower them with the baptism of the Holy Spirit to replicate His earthly ministry exactly. They fundamentally denied the very essence of Christianity, which was *"the power of God unto salvation"* (Rom. 1:16 KJV). By contrast, we see that the introduction of the Kingdom of God—that is, the rule of the Spirit—is clearly the essence of Jesus's mission and message. Jesus came to do the following:[4]

- **Introduce** the Kingdom/New Covenant Spirit;[5]

- **Model** a perfect example of how to live out that Kingdom/New Covenant Spirit in a ministry of revelation and power. *"I have given you an example, that* [you] *also should do as I have done to you"* (John 13:15 KJV);[6]

- **Commission** to the disciples His Kingdom mission, expecting them to replicate its content and method;[7]

- **Ratify** (place His signature on) the Kingdom/New Covenant Spirit in His blood[8] (the cross had purpose beyond "forgiveness of sins": Jesus's death on the cross was for those who had broken the covenant of refusing the covenant of hearing God's voice, and then offering this covenant anew;

- **Vindicate** the Kingdom/New Covenant in the power of His resurrection;[9]

- **Bestow** the Kingdom/New Covenant Spirit from Heaven;[10] and, ultimately...

- **Become** the New Covenant Spirit in that He is "with us always, even to the ends of the earth" (see Matt. 28:20).[11]

We can see, then, how so much of the later discussion about the baptism and spiritual gifts of the Holy Spirit centered on the following questions: How does the baptism in the Holy Spirit relate to "salvation"? Where does it fit into the *ordo salutis*? Does this experience, which seemed undeniable, become part of salvation, or is it something subsequent to it? Early Pentecostals, being good Protestants, decided that the baptism came in the *ordo salutis* after regeneration. However, because in their experience it resulted from "tarrying" in much piety and prayer, semiconsciously some assigned it to the stage of sanctification. Others thought that the baptism of the Holy Spirit was sanctification—an experience of instantaneous holiness.

Furthermore, because the baptism entailed a miracle or the conferral of a spiritual gift, then it must "prove" a doctrine. Well, what doctrine could it evidence? Just as Catholic saints were "accredited" by miracles, so these Protestants came to believe that they were "accredited" by these miraculous spiritual gifts (tongues) as "evidence" of having received the Spirit. This fascination with evidence may have derived from the philosophical climate of the Enlightenment, as when theologian Jonathan Edwards sought the scientific "marks" of genuine revival as proof against critics of the Great Awakening in the 1700s. The Bible, however, has scant interest in issues

135

like evidence and subsequence simply because it focuses on a different notion of salvation and what that salvation looks like.

The Baptism of the Spirit as Jesus Intended

To get at the emphasis of Jesus's mission, we need only to see how He was introduced for the first time in all four Gospels. John the Baptist, in preparing for Jesus, said, *"I baptize you with water for repentance, but He who is coming after me is mightier than I...He will baptize you with the Holy Spirit"* (Matt. 3:11 ESV).[12] When we introduce someone for the first time, we try to associate the person with his or her most important or notable feature, don't we? Jesus's most notable feature, then, according to the New Testament, is that He baptizes in the Holy Spirit. Why must we stress this? Because if you believe traditional theology (either Catholic or Protestant), that is certainly not the way you would introduce Jesus. You would say, "He will die on the cross for your sins!" True, but when we review the accounts of Jesus's ministry in the New Testament, we see summaries like the following:

- *The Son of Man did not come to be served, but to serve, and to give His life as a ransom for many* (Matthew 20:28; Mark 10:45).[13]

- *Look, the Lamb of God, who takes away the sin of the world!* (John 1:29)

- *The reason the Son of God appeared was to destroy the devil's work* (1 John 3:8).

- *Here is a trustworthy saying that deserves full acceptance: Christ Jesus came into the world to save sinners—of whom I am the worst* (1 Timothy 1:15).

All of these Scriptures appear to support the Protestant notion that Jesus's mission was only to "save sinners" from sins—the mission of the Catholic Mass. But the bigger picture is that Jesus saved sinners as part of His central mission to inaugurate a New Covenant of the Spirit.

The Scriptures above focus on the immediate need to repent and then be immersed in the Spirit as the same kind of empowered disciples Jesus had been training for three years on earth. His goal for them is clear when He commissions them in Matthew 10, Mark 6, and Luke 9 and 10 and then later recapitulates these directives in the so-called "Great Commission" in Matthew 28:19-20. Nevertheless, He also showed His main goal as being filled with the Spirit in order to fulfill the "Gospel" as the disciples had already demonstrated in their "midterm exams" (in Matthew, Mark, and Luke above) in the earlier commissioning accounts in the Gospels. Paul can be seen as a faithful disciple who operates in the New Covenant Spirit because he "fulfills" the Gospel in Holy Spirit power. Look carefully at this more faithful translation of Romans 15:18-20:

> For I will not venture to speak of anything except what Christ has accomplished through me to bring the Gentiles to obedience—by word and deed, by the power of signs and wonders, by the power of the Spirit of God—so that from Jerusalem and all the way around to Illyricum I have fulfilled [the ministry of] the gospel of Christ; and thus I make it my ambition [to preach the] gospel... (Romans 15:18–20 ESV).

The words in brackets in this typical Evangelical translation (ESV) do not appear in the original Greek text. It shows how the Protestant translators thought that the Gospel must be primarily a verbal, creedal recital, rather than what the text says. Paul says, "I fulfilled the Gospel of Christ" and "I make it my ambition to evangelize, or gospelize." There is no word for *preach* in this verse. "Word and deed" was an old rabbinic term that meant "prophecy and miracle" and was used in reference to a prophet.[14] In other words, the Gospel itself was not proven by miracles, but the disciples presented the Gospel. Signs and wonders (charismata), by the power of the Spirit of God, expressed the Gospel—that is, Paul "evangelized" in that way. Yes, he did explain what was happening in words, but he indicated that he was fulfilling Jesus's earlier commissions to His disciples in the Gospels by performing healings and exorcisms. He, along with the other disciples, used these powerful acts to explain that *"the Kingdom of God has come to you"* (Luke 11:20 GW). Here God revealed Himself—"bore witness"—as He characteristically does—in power, as in Second Corinthians 12:12, First Thessalonians 1:5, Hebrews 2:4, and the passage above.

Why, when the Scriptures are so clear about the centrality of the baptism of the Spirit to Jesus's mission, is there this disconnect about the nature of the Gospel? Well, in the early 1500s, theologians were fighting a life-and-death struggle over the question "How much does it cost to go to Heaven?" The Catholics were charging money to get people out of purgatory, while the Reformers were trying to show that salvation is free because of the death of Jesus on the cross. As a result, all traditional theology for the last 500 years has been centered on this issue rather than what the Gospels clearly and explicitly taught about Jesus—that He came to "baptize in the Holy Spirit." At this point, we need to understand where the Bible places the very important event of the cross.

Chapter 10

WHERE IS THE CROSS OF JESUS IN ALL OF THIS?

The cross of Jesus—His sacrifice for our sins—is of central importance for the baptism of the Holy Spirit. How? The cross was God's way of "paying for" the sins that led to a broken covenant, which then resulted in all the penalties listed in Deuteronomy 28: sickness, oppression, catastrophe, ruined lives, etc. (see Deut. 28:15-68). God temporarily offered animal sacrifices, ritual purifications, the written Law, the Day of Atonement, etc., as ways to get His people to recognize the seriousness of their sin and to listen to His voice again.

When Jesus died on the cross, just as once an animal sacrifice reminded the covenant-breaker of his sin, now that price was paid once and for all. An animal sacrifice was to renew the Old Covenant. Jesus's death, however, was not only to pay for the broken Old Covenant, but it was also to introduce a totally different way of relating to God—a New Covenant, where the only "law" was to hear God's voice directly—not a whole bunch of New Testament rules, though these "rules" do not contradict the true voice of God speaking directly into our hearts.[1]

The Book of Hebrews is explicit about the cross and the covenant: the cross mediated the New Covenant; it was not the New

Covenant itself (see Heb. 8:6). When Jesus said, *"This is the new covenant in My blood,"* He is saying that this blood is ratifying, or "signing in blood," a New Covenant (Luke 22:20). His blood on the cross "signs the contract"; that is, He establishes the new contract/covenant as legally valid and binding. But this "signature" was not the New Covenant itself. The New Covenant was the thing ratified—the charismatic Spirit.[2] If there's no cross, the New Covenant remains an unsigned document, not relevant or applicable to anyone.

This is the very argument Paul uses against the Corinthian elitists who were so much "in the Spirit" that they didn't recognize that they were breaking the covenant by ignoring what the covenant really was—the operation of the Spirit in His giftings, especially among the poor, whom the elitists were ignoring and shunning. The "Body" of Jesus is described clearly in the context (see 1 Cor. 12:12). He was not referring to a wafer or a piece of bread, except that it was "broken," just as the Corinthian church was broken by excluding Spirit-filled poor Christians who were in the New Covenant of the Spirit (see Isa. 59:21). Having denied the voice and power of God in these people, the elite came under the judgment of a broken covenant: *"That is why many of you are weak and ill, and some have died"* (1 Cor. 11:30 ESV).[3] They were under judgment because they denied the power and presence of the Holy Spirit in others and in so doing denied the cross and sacrifice of Jesus to inaugurate that New Covenant of the Spirit.[4]

Hebrews makes this same point even more powerfully. It states in five different ways what a "broken covenant" looks like and how serious it is:

> *For it is impossible, in the case of those who have once been enlightened, who have tasted the heavenly gift, and have shared in the Holy Spirit, and have tasted the goodness of the word of God and the powers of the age to come, and then have fallen away, to restore them again to repentance, since they are crucifying once again the*

Son of God to their own harm and holding Him up to
contempt. For land that has drunk the rain that often
falls on it, and produces a crop useful to those for whose
sake it is cultivated, receives a blessing from God. But if it
bears thorns and thistles, it is worthless and near to being
cursed, and its end is to be burned (Hebrews 6:4-8).

Starting with "enlightened," there are four more ways of describing the New Covenant of the Spirit: *"heavenly gift...Holy Spirit...goodness of the word of God and the powers of the age to come* [heavenly power]*"* (Heb. 6:4-5). This is not talking about traditional salvation. It is talking about the manifestations of the Holy Spirit! If this "Word" or Spirit is rejected or renounced, it means the same thing as First Corinthians 11: the meaning of the cross, which, at terrible cost, bought us God's greatest gift—the gift of Jesus Himself in the Spirit, His presence, love, revelation and power—is being denied. To deny that greatest gift is to sneer at and dismiss the terrible suffering of Jesus and His shed blood. Note the analogy in this passage involving the land: if the land has received heavenly rain but does not produce what God intended, it is *"cursed, and its end is to be burned"* (Heb. 6:8). A cessationist who denies the baptism of the New Covenant Spirit has a very serious problem. "Well," you might ask, "didn't Jesus die on the cross to save us from sin?" Of course, but why did He do that?

Theologians, then, in the heat of scholarly battle, changed the meaning of many other words with which we think we are familiar. For example, in order to find their central *ordo salutis* in the New Testament, they changed "grace" from its New Testament meaning of "generous Spirit empowerment" to "mercy," because in their system, the charis-charismata ("grace"-"grace things"—spiritual gifts) connection had no relevance. Ditto for "faith," which moved from signifying "response to revelation/assurance," often for healing, to "assent/agreement to a doctrine of salvation."

Another important term, "Kingdom of God" or "Kingdom of Heaven," which was the central theme of Jesus's ministry, was all but ignored by traditional theology and, incredibly, was redefined as the "invisible church" of true believers. The Kingdom is a huge theme in the New Testament, and its essence is *dunamis* ("miracle power" in First Corinthians 4:20) and is a virtual synonym for "Holy Spirit."[5] We have already mentioned how the term "Holy Spirit" has been restricted in Protestant theology by their idea of salvation. But how does the Bible describe the baptism in the Holy Spirit? Let's break down the two terms in this concept—*baptism* and *Holy Spirit*.

Baptism has received sustained scholarly attention throughout the church era because it has traditionally been seen as a familiar ritual involving "salvation." Recent scholarship has shown that Christian baptism seems to have been derived from the early Jewish practice of washings, that is, ceremonial purification—a symbol of the forgiveness of sins when one repented. John the Baptist emphasized preparation to receive the Kingdom/Spirit: "I baptize in water, but One mightier than I will baptize you in the Holy Spirit" (see Luke 3:16). When Jesus was baptized, He didn't need to be cleansed of sin but to *"fulfill all righteousness"* (Matt. 3:15), probably meaning to offer an example to all others.

This same pattern is followed on the Day of Pentecost when Peter answers the anxious question, *"What shall we do?"* (Acts 2:37) asked by those shocked that they had crucified the One now pouring out the Spirit in fire, thunder and shaking as at the Sinai covenant. The answer was: *"Repent and be baptized...in the name* [authority] *of Jesus Christ for the forgiveness of your sins. And you will receive the gift of the Holy Spirit"* (Acts 2:38).

Do these two examples demonstrate being "baptized in the Holy Spirit," or do they mean more narrowly that one is "immersed" or "washed" in the Holy Spirit—an event in which one can sense a "pouring" over one's body? Maybe both? *It is clear that the New Testament is not interested in establishing a ritual but a reality.*[6] Therefore, this event may appear in the New Testament as many different ways of experiencing the Spirit.

Holy Spirit is a term that has been radically changed from its original biblical usage.[7] Whereas traditional theology mostly limits the Holy Spirit to the topics of the Trinity and salvation, a thorough, disciplined statistical study of the contexts for each occurrence of the Spirit of God in the Old and New Testaments shows that the terms for divine Spirit were overwhelmingly associated with prophetic revelation and utterance, as well as miraculous power,[8] a view that is the consensus of biblical (but not systematic) theologians.[9] Of course, because all this revelation and power ceased, the traditionalists were forced to deny the present relevance to them of this New Testament charismatic portrayal of the Spirit. Most modern texts of systematic theology still minimize it: they just don't seem to be "into" biblical scholarship and understanding the Spirit the way Jesus and the apostles did (and as over 700 million Christians do today).

The bottom line, then, is that if we combine these terms, *baptism* and *Holy Spirit*, it seems that the New Testament concept of the baptism in/with/of the Holy Spirit is that one is "immersed or flooded into the power and gifts of God, particularly gifts of revelation, prophecy, utterance, and power."

Why Is the Baptism of the Holy Spirit Central to Christianity?

The baptism in the Holy Spirit is not simply an "add-on" or an expendable "frosting on the cake" to one's salvation. This is not a biblical idea. In practice, all Christians—indeed, all people—have received revelation, or "the voice" of God (see Rom. 1:18). No one can even come to Christ "except the Spirit draw him" (see John 6:44). Even most cessationists will violate their own theology when they say they receive impressions, "words" from God, or remarkable answers to prayer. They simply re-label these experiences. Instead of a "word of knowledge," they will say, "I sensed that God was leading me to…" Or, instead of naming something "prophecy," they might say, "That person spoke with 'divine grace,'" which is the same thing. Still, traditional theology has a distinct dampening effect on the overt work of the Spirit. People under this theology tend to be skeptical and negative about spiritual gifts.

Despite the denials of traditional theology, at least 38 percent of Americans, according to a 2013 poll, "have done something because God told them to."[10] Perhaps because it is based on real-life human experience, belief in miracles has become an accepted part of popular culture. A 2003 Harris poll, for instance, revealed that 84 percent of the public believed that miracles occur in today's world.[11] A 2005 Harris poll indicated that 73 percent of adults believed in miracles.[12] In 2004, a poll of 1,100 physicians revealed that 74 percent believed that miracles occurred in the past and, even more interestingly, that 73 percent agreed that miracles occur today. A surprising number—55 percent—of the physicians claimed to witness medical miracles in their practice.[13] What all of these statistics indicate is that the biblical "word of power" has taken deep root in most of the world because spiritual discernment is a "natural" part of mankind. The Bible says that even the universal human conscience is revealed from God: we know right from wrong by God's "voice."[14]

The "voice of God" theme is big in the world. Everybody hears from God, but that is not quite the same thing as the baptism in the Holy Spirit. Why? The baptism is not simply a matter of hearing and uttering God's word of power on occasion but it involves "walking in the Spirit," being "immersed" and "flooded" with the presence of the "speaking, empowering" Spirit, ideally (but rarely) on a continuing basis. Put another way, this is the intense presence of Jesus, who "will be with you to the end of the age."[15] This continual living in the Spirit of revelation, prophecy, and power is the ideal state of the Christian disciple. It is the answer to Moses's desire:

"I wish that all the Lord's people were prophets" (Num. 11:29, echoed in 1 Cor. 14:1,5). "How is all of this reflected in the 'big picture' of the Bible?" you ask. Let's examine that question.

The Baptism in the Spirit Is the Ultimate Expression of the Central Human Experience of the Bible: Hearing and Uttering God's Voice

The question often arises: Why do Pentecostals emphasize the "evidence" of speech (usually speaking in tongues) in connection with the baptism of the Holy Spirit? The answer is, probably because the Bible emphasizes a God who speaks and the connection between the Holy Spirit and prophecy (revealed utterance). Our short answer is to note Luke's title to the Pentecost narrative, "When the Holiday of Pentecost Was Fulfilled."[16] Pentecost was a Jewish holiday that celebrated the giving of the covenant on Sinai. Peter's speech lays out the foundational structure of the Old and New Covenant with the world. If there was any place that the speaker needed to "get it right" it was in the most important keynote address of all of Christianity as found in Acts 2.

The "punch line" of the Pentecost speech—that which captured the speech's entire purpose—was a reference to Isaiah 59:21, which summarizes and "fulfills" the whole narrative of Acts 2, which is a citation of verse 39. The point of the Pentecost story is that the New Covenant is the Spirit of prophecy (speech) equipping disciples for the mission Jesus demonstrated and then gave to them. But what exactly was that covenant? It's not what we have traditionally believed it to be.

> *"As for me, this is my covenant with them," says the Lord. "My Spirit, who is on you, and my words that I have put in your mouth will not depart from your mouth, or from the mouths of your children, or from the mouths of their descendants from this time on and forever"* (Isaiah 59:21).

145

Totally contrary to traditional, cessationist theology, the great revelation here is Luke saying that the New Covenant is that the Spirit will come upon both "You" (singular = Jesus) and upon your "children" (disciples) forever and that the prophetic words that the Spirit gives will never depart from them. The Book of Hebrews makes the same point. The thesis statement of Hebrews is 1:1-2, *"He has [now] spoken...by His Son"* (Heb. 1:2). The rest of Hebrews emphasizes the centrality of Jesus as the mediator of the New Covenant, which is immediate revelation—the teaching (Law) written in the heart (see Heb. 12:24). Three times the reader is reminded, "Today when you hear His [Jesus's] voice..."

Hebrews concludes with a contrast of the Old Covenant, when the Israelites were too terrified to receive God's voice (and chose a book instead), against the New Covenant of the Spirit, which came with rejoicing.[17] The punch line of this narrative is, "Therefore, do not refuse the One who speaks!" (see Heb. 12:25). The Book of Hebrews, then, is about the New Covenant of revelation as described in Jeremiah 31:33: the law written on the heart.

Paul also lays out the relationship between the two covenants in detail in Second Corinthians 3. According to him, the Old Covenant is God revealing Himself first through "speech" (rejected) and then through writing, which Paul sees as an inferior substitute for God's voice (see 2 Cor. 3:7-11).[18]

Note that the original offer was God's speaking directly to them.[19] The superior New Covenant involves the Spirit revealing God's word directly into one's innermost being (see Jer. 31:33) or into the mouth (see Isa. 59:21; Acts 2:39). If we imitate Paul, as we're told to do (see 1 Cor. 11:1; 2 Thess. 3:7,9), then we are to be *"ministers of a new covenant—not of the letter* [expounding texts and traditions] *but of the Spirit* [conveying God's immediate revelation, prophecy and power]*"* (2 Cor. 3:6). The Pentecost event was the first time this Old/New Covenant offer was fulfilled. It was fulfilled by the Spirit baptism revealing God via speech.

Chapter 11

A Review of the Rest of the Bible's Themes' Relation to the Baptism of the Holy Spirit

Let's back up and quickly survey the major themes concerning the prophetic word of power in the Bible: creation, the core temptation, the plot lines of the biblical narratives, and the mission of Jesus, which He commissioned to His disciples (us). We have already discussed the Old and New Covenants. All these themes can shed light on the nature of the Holy Spirit baptism.

Creation sets the agenda for the whole Bible. The message of Genesis 1 is "here's how the universe began and is sustained." By implication, since we are part of that creation, our own lives are sustained as well. How? By the mighty word of God—both in the powerful word of creation, but also, like God Himself, by acknowledging that word and affirming its creation. Note the pattern: on each "day,"

- God utters the powerful, intelligent creative word;

- a huge miracle of a stage in creation occurs;

- and then God verbally "names" it (thereby acknowledging it) or affirms it as "good."

So, like all creation, our life is sustained by the mighty words of God that we also utter. This is characteristic of the baptism in the Holy Spirit.

Because Adam was made "in the image and likeness of God" (see Gen. 1:27), the characteristic "word" came from his mouth when he was to "name" the animals (or acknowledge, as even God did, God's mighty works in creation). It is interesting that at Pentecost, at their baptism, the disciples' tongues were "recounting the mighty works of God" (see Acts 2:11).

This "naming/acknowledging" carries the idea of an artist stepping back to admire the work of his hands and of his son doing likewise. Furthermore, it connotes a rejoicing about a conquest over the forces of darkness and nothingness. No wonder there is such contention today over teaching creationism in schools!

Adam was created for three actions:

- **To Be Intimate with God.** Just as Eve was made of the same "stuff" as Adam, so Adam and Eve were made "in the image and likeness" of God—to communicate in love and freedom (see Gen. 1:27).

- **To Proclaim** over creation in "naming" the animals (praise of mighty works?).

- **To Take Authority** over all creation; to "work" and "guard" the Garden against the serpent, the demonic, although the enemy is not made clear until Genesis 3.

The first step, "intimacy," resulted in the other two steps—the result of God's "breath" (Spirit) within them. Here we have the elements of the baptism of the Holy Spirit: an infusion of God's own Spirit/breath/life to bring Adam to life; then, with God's life/wisdom, Adam could proclaim the mighty word over creation and take authority to manage and protect it. All of this is a prototype experience of the baptism of the Holy Spirit.

The Prototype Baptism of the Spirit in All the Role Models of the Bible

Sixty percent of the Bible, both Old and New Testaments, appears in the form of story or narrative. It is remarkable that the plot lines of these stories are all the same: God speaks to a person about doing something unusual for Him. The man (usually) accepts the "word" and soon suffers serious resistance for obeying it. Often there is a huge gap between a promise and its fulfillment, stretching the faith of our "role model" to incredible limits. We can think here of Noah, Abraham, Jacob, Joseph, Moses, the judges, prophets, and others. Hebrews 11 gives us a longer list of those who had faith and were stretched to the limit. The Bible seems to be making the point that if these men of faith could put up with so much for so long, you should be able to do less than that. What kept these guys going for so long under such unfulfilled anxiety and pressure? They clearly heard God's voice, they remained in contact with Him daily (see Isa. 50:4), and, above all, they lived a life of faith, with "faith" being defined as "assurance"—the voice of God saying that something is to be and then being empowered by God to respond to that "word" against all kinds of resistance. A gift of faith is like a mini-baptism—the "word" or Spirit of God speaking and empowering you for a task.

Like Adam, at God's mighty, creative "word," we almost reflexively respond in some sort of Spirit-driven exclamation: laughter, praise, the narration of His mighty works, prophecy, or speaking in tongues—or any combination thereof.

Often when people of God encountered His presence, they shook or fell down before Him. Scoffers criticize revivals when people "fall down," saying that it is humiliating and undignified. Exactly! No one enters the presence of God without losing all pride. To experience God truly, we will immediately fall on our face before His majesty and glory; we will sense that we are only dust before Him. To scoff at this only shows an unwillingness to enter God's presence.

The scoffers at Pentecost quite likely saw at least some of the 120 as "falling down drunk," a phenomenon associated with almost all of the major revivals in Church history, though they used it as an excuse to accuse the 120 of shameful drunkenness.

Is it accidental that those movements in which people allowed themselves to be "humiliated" before the Lord in this way typically grew and prospered over time, while the "religiously correct" scoffers tended to wither? This pattern is confirmed when we examine the somewhat detailed "callings" of the major Old Testament prophets. Each of the three major prophets—Isaiah, Jeremiah, and Ezekiel—describes his quite similar calling, which, in each case, resembled the events of Pentecost. By contrast, the Pentecost group had already received their instructions; Pentecost completed the experience, the "prophetic call." Obviously, if the 120 at Pentecost were to have the prophet's mission, they needed the Spirit of prophecy. The Old Testament prophets simply accepted the original offer of the Old Covenant at Sinai: the voice of God, which, though it was fearfully presented, was received this time by the prophet.[1] The same fear-inducing phenomena were found at Pentecost: shaking, thunderous noise, fire, and prophetic response. The "call" on these prophets remarkably shared several characteristics that resemble the baptism of the Holy Spirit and what happened to those early Christians afterward:[2]

- First is the contrast of the glory of God and the human weakness of the prospective prophet.[3] There is shaking, thunder, and a spectacular show of light and glory.

- Second is the cleansing of the lips, expressing that the message is holy, that is, separated from human contamination.[4]

- Third, the prophet "speaks out" in response to God's powerful presence.[5]

- Fourth, the prophet is told not to be afraid of those to whom he is sent.[6]

- Fifth, God indicates that the prophet will not necessarily experience success—at least in the short term.[7]

- Sixth, the central point is: "the Word of the Lord" comes to these prophets.[8] There is no confusion that it is God who is speaking to them.[9]

All the prophets were sent to guide Israel away from failure and toward listening to God's voice—an experience of the Holy Spirit, the "Word of the Lord." Throughout Acts we notice the repetition of the phrase "the Word of the Lord grew and multiplied" as a way of dividing the book into stages.

It is important to note, however, that the revelatory experiences of these prophets are quite different, even though they share these themes. Accordingly, people today will experience a variety of revelation experiences that accompany God's calling: dreams, visions, impressions, audible voices, words from others sent from God, circumstances, healings, miracles, special provisions, financial blessings, etc. Some may experience something like this only once or a handful of times in their life. Some today will confuse the present passive verb *filled* with a past tense verb: "Are you Spirit filled?" "Yes, I was Spirit filled in 1958!" Most believe that a "filling" of the Holy Spirit needs to be continually upgraded—that one can't assume permanence, like the doctrine of "once saved, always saved."[10]

Indeed, just like the baptism of the Holy Spirit, the old nation of Israel was called by God's voice for the specific task of being "sanctified"—that is, not just to be "good," but to become priests who heard God's voice to then give it to the inquirer and, indeed, to all nations. Here is Israel's "calling":

You yourselves have seen what I did to the Egyptians [miracles], *and how I bore you on eagles' wings, and brought you to Myself. Now then, if you will indeed obey My voice and keep My covenant* [which originally was the offer of His voice] *then you shall be My own possession among all the peoples, for all the earth is Mine; and you shall be to Me a kingdom of priests* [whose main job was to "inquire of the Lord" for people] *and a holy nation* (Exodus 19:4-6 NASB).

A "holy" nation meant that it was "sanctified" in the sense of being "made into a priest" who "inquired of the Lord for His 'Word.'" Just like the person experiencing the baptism of the Holy Spirit, the priest was both to hear and utter God's revealed word, essentially as a prophecy, or a "word of knowledge/word of wisdom" by the revelation of the Spirit.

So throughout Israel's history, many had experiences very much like what had happened at Pentecost. But as the Bible tells us, these experiences were intermittent and sometimes rare: *"We do not see our signs; there is no longer any prophet, and there is none among us who knows how long"* (Ps. 74:9 ESV). Nevertheless, some held out hope: *"I stand in awe of Your deeds, Lord. Repeat them in our day, in our time make them known"* (Hab. 3:2). Jeremiah, for his part, seems more positive, seeing a continuity of miracles not only in Israel but all over the world (see Jer. 32:20). The New Testament/ New Covenant era is characterized by the permanent outflow of the charismatic Spirit. But when you think about it, Israel's experiences with the Spirit may not have been so different than those of today after all!

Summary of the Old Testament Prototypes of the Baptism in the Spirit

With the Old Testament emphasis on the mighty word of God—beginning in Genesis with the creation story, continuing with the presentation of the major figures offered as role models for the readers, and extending into the discussion of the prophets as the ideal among the Lord's people (see Num. 11:29)—we have a great many cases expressing the major elements of the baptism of the Holy Spirit and answering the "why" of its association with prophetic speech.

God's servants—the true role models—were always equipped with the gift of being able to hear God's voice, sense His presence, and prophesy God's love and authority over individuals and nations. This is the way the baptism is experienced and expressed: in speech and the resulting power, with the goal of discipling the nations.

The Purpose of the Baptism in the Holy Spirit (The Center of the Gospel)

By receiving the baptism of the Holy Spirit we are enabled to:

- Fulfill the central pattern of creation: we have our being in God's mighty voice;

- Overcome the "primal temptation" of the serpent's false knowledge by heeding the voice of God;

- Learn the main life lesson of God's role models, the patriarchs and prophets;

- Fulfill the mission of Israel to hear His voice and be a *"light for the nations"* (Isa. 49:6 ESV);

- Fulfill the central mission of Jesus to *"baptize you with the Holy Spirit"* (Matt. 3:11; Luke 3:16);

- Fulfill the New Covenant of the Spirit poured out at Pentecost and beyond;

- And fulfill the specific commissions given to all disciples of Jesus.

In other words, in the baptism we fulfill the one objective that the whole Bible wants from us!

True Discipleship as Jesus Taught It Involves the Baptism in the Spirit

What exactly did Jesus emphasize when training His disciples, and why is it so unclear to us today? Let's begin with the second part of the question: the reason why the clear commissions to the disciples to perform acts of healing, proclaim the Kingdom, and live minimally by faith are unclear is because for most of Church history, politically powerful leaders felt shamed by their inability and unwillingness to apply these commissions to themselves and resentful of those few ordinary people in the Church who were actually trying to do so. The easy answer, then, for Church leaders was simply to claim that *those commands applied only to the original apostles* and that the commands are not for today. That unbiblical excuse got them off the hook and contaminated Church theology for almost all of its history. With the explosion of the worldwide Charismatic renewal in the last 100 years, where millions have active ministries in spiritual gifts, this old excuse to ignore Jesus's early commissionings to the disciples is harder to accept.

The Pattern Is Jesus

Traditional Christian theology and its understanding of discipleship has given us the impression that we could never imitate Jesus because He was God (and we aren't) and that He therefore performed miracles only to prove that He was God. So if we try to do miracles, healings, or spiritual gifts, we are blaspheming because we are thereby claiming to be God.[11] It was permissible to "imitate" Christ, but only in acts of piety, ethics, traditional ministry, and suffering.[12] This is bad theology, and it is not biblical.

By contrast, Jesus explicitly follows the pattern of training rabbis in His time when He affirms, *"A pupil is not above his teacher* [rabbi], *but everyone* [without exception], *after he has been fully trained, will be* [exactly] *like his teacher"* (Luke 6:40 NASB). This pattern of rigidity in replicating Jesus's life is repeated in John 13:34; 17:18,23;

and 20:21 using the conceptual formula, "As I did…so you." In John 13:15, Jesus states, *"For I gave you an example that you also should do* [exactly] *as I did"* (NASB). The continuation and replication of Jesus's mission in His disciples is explicit in John 20:21: *"[Exactly] as the Father has sent Me, I also send you"* (NASB).

Paul requires of his readers: *"Be imitators of me,* [exactly] *as I am of Christ"* (1 Cor. 11:1). First Thessalonians 1:5-8 shows that Paul expected his followers to mimic the way that he presented the Gospel in power, as in Romans 15:18-19 and Second Corinthians 12:12:

> *Our gospel came to you not only in word, but also in power and in the Holy Spirit and with full conviction. You know what kind of men we proved to be among you for your sake. And you became **imitators** of us and of the Lord, for you received the word in much affliction, with the joy of the Holy Spirit, so that you became an example to all the believers in Macedonia and in Achaia. For not only has the word of the Lord sounded forth from you in Macedonia and Achaia, but your faith in God has gone forth everywhere, so that we need not say anything* (1 Thessalonians 1:5-8 ESV).

For lack of space, I cannot develop the New Testament evidence to show this imitation pattern in discipleship. I would refer you to my article "The 'Imitation of Christ' in Christian Tradition: Its Missing Charismatic Evidence" and the last section (on discipleship) in my book *What's Wrong with Protestant Theology?* All through the Gospels, the disciples were encouraged to emulate Jesus as He modeled His healing and deliverance ministry. However, nowhere is He more specific and direct about this as when He sent them out to do this ministry by themselves, without Him. These early commissioning accounts represent an important step in their training and showed precisely what form He expected their ministry to take. They also show the reader what form of Christian ministry should be considered "normal."

But, we need to take one step back and take a look at the breath-taking, extremist, and radical mission that Jesus gave to His disciples. It was not to find a church, hire a worship leader, and assemble a congregation. In fact, it was the same essential mission that He gave to Adam, the prophets, and all who have ever followed God: *"And He appointed twelve (whom He also named apostles* [the "new Israel" or people of God]*) so that they might be with Him and He might send them out to preach* [proclaim/announce the Kingdom] *and have authority to cast out demons"* (Mark 3:14-15 ESV).

That's It—the Universal Commission!

The baptism of the Holy Spirit was to empower the disciples to fulfill this simple but profound commission. They were told to wait "in the city"—"in Jerusalem"—in order to fulfill the prophecy, "for He comes like a mighty, rushing torrent, driven by the Spirit, a redeemer to Zion [Jerusalem] for repentance to Jacob [Israel, God's people]." Then they would see the fulfillment of Isaiah 59:21 in the New Covenant, the goal of the Bible and the central purpose of Jesus's mission: to baptize in the Holy Spirit.

The baptism was to empower fully what they had already been instructed repeatedly to do (Acts 1:8).[13] Typical of these instructions is Luke 9: *"And He called the twelve together and gave them power and authority over all demons and to cure diseases, and He sent them out to proclaim the kingdom of God and to heal"* (Luke 9:1-2 ESV).

The disciples also were told to "live off the land," to live minimally, and essentially to trust God not only for healings and deliverances, but also for their daily bread and housing. We Charismatics tend to downplay this latter part of the commissions.

It is important to note that not only the 12, but the 70 (representing all nations) were given these basic instructions on how to present what were the essentials of Christianity—the very way the Gospel was to be presented. Remember, the power and the dependence on God for provision did not "prove" the Gospel; *it is the*

Gospel. These commissions express exactly what Jesus came to bring: *"the kingdom of God* [that] *does not consist in talk but in* [miracle] *power"* (1 Cor. 4:20 ESV).

Conclusion

Traditional theology sees "salvation" as the process of being "made righteous" (justified) from the penalties of "sins" (plural) and as involving regeneration with sanctification, which minimizes sins thereafter to help one reach Heaven. Traditional Pentecostals and Charismatics expand the "sanctification" stage to include the baptism (for Pentecostals, the first time one speaks in tongues; for Charismatics, a variety of spiritual experiences and/or gifts). Both groups see the baptism of the Holy Spirit as "empowering for service," but historically, as things cool off, they often uneasily regress to the default experience and theology of traditional "salvation," often, in practice, relegating the baptism to a warm memory in their past.

The New Testament sees "sins" as all expressing the sin, that is, not "walking in the Spirit"—denying the charismatic experience of hearing God's voice in His gifts. The answer to "sins" in this life is not simply to stop sinning but to "walk in the Spirit." That is what Hebrews 6:5-6 is all about. Denying the voice and work of the Spirit is blaspheming the Holy Spirit.[14] If one refuses to hear God's revealing voice, one necessarily cannot respond and be redeemed.

Avoiding hell and attaining Heaven, of course, is the ultimate goal, but unlike traditional theology, which focuses on being "saved" for these goals and behaving as ethical churchgoers in the meantime, the focus of the New Testament is on the "here and now": What is God's mission for us in this life? Traditional theology about the cross focuses on the sacrifice of Christ as payment for our sins so that we can avoid hell, attain Heaven, and try to sin less in the meantime. This is the essence of the Catholic Mass ("the source and summit of the Christian life") and of the Protestant version of the mass, the *ordo salutis* (stages of salvation, also the end point of the

Christian life). In this, traditional theology minimizes the purposes of the cross. The New Testament view, however, is much bigger: the cross was not only to abrogate the broken Old Covenant (forgiveness of sins), but it was *also* to ratify the New Covenant, which is the *Spirit of prophecy and power* ("word and deed" [see Luke 24:19; Rom. 15:18]) made available for all.[15]

Traditional theology either ignores or denies this prophecy and power component ("cessationism"), which is actually *central* to the New Covenant! The mission of Jesus, as introduced prominently in all four Gospels, is to "baptize in the Holy Spirit"—in other words, to commission and empower all disciples to replicate His Kingdom mission "in power" *as He spent years training them to do.*[16] Paul *explicitly describes* the nature of the Gospel in Romans 15:18-19 as being "fulfilled" (not "fully preached/proclaimed") by the *"power of signs and wonders, by the power of the Spirit of God"* (Rom. 15:19 ESV). He says that the essence of the Kingdom of God (which Jesus came to bring) is "not talk, but *dunamis* (miracle power)" (see 1 Cor. 4:20). Paul also accurately predicted a traditional theology that would "have a form of godliness, but deny its *dunamis*" (see 2 Tim. 3:5). So the New Testament is clear: the all-important, indispensable cross *ratified* or *mediated* the New Covenant, but the cross is not the New Covenant itself.[17] The New Covenant Spirit of prophecy and power for all (see 1 Cor. 12:6) is the goal and end result of Jesus's stated mission to baptize in the Holy Spirit.[18] Thus the cross now *fully* expresses its great act of love, not simply to forgive sins, but to be expressed in *powerful acts of loving compassion*—in healing, deliverance from demons, and oppression. *"For this purpose the Son of God was manifested, that He might destroy the works of the devil"* (1 John 3:8 KJV).

The New Covenant is explicitly described as the Holy Spirit characterized as prophetic revelation[19] or revealing presence.[20] The New Covenant Spirit comes upon the Messiah first in revelation and power and from Him onto His "children."[21] All four Gospels introduce Jesus's mission in the same way: to "baptize in the Holy Spirit."[22] Jesus refers to the *"new covenant in My blood,"* which requires "discerning the 'Body'"—the charismatic community (Luke 22:20; see 1 Cor. 12:12). This baptism "into one Body" is the reception of the charismatic Spirit to empower followers of Jesus to replicate His earthly ministry in power.[23]

By contrast, the New Testament itself defines the New Covenant clearly and very differently in Second Corinthians 3; Hebrews 8–12, especially 12:18-25; Acts 2:39, which very clearly cites Isaiah 59:21 (*"This is My covenant with them"* [Isa. 59:21] —the gift of the charismatic Spirit of prophecy, the powerful "Word" going forth); and many other places. The baptism of the Holy Spirit is the New Covenant experienced. This continuing experience represents, as we have seen, the very goal of the Bible and the central mission of Jesus: to baptize in the Holy Spirit—as He is introduced in all four Gospels.

The New Covenant, then, is the charismatic, prophetic Spirit empowering and commissioning the ideal "child/servant of God." Specifically, the mission and message of Jesus is to make disciples who are "imitators" and "followers" of Him (see Mark 3:14-15)— disciples who are created for the same purpose as was "Adam" (mankind): (1) to be "with Him"; (2) to "proclaim" (the mighty, creative "Word" of life and power); and (3) to have (delegated) authority over all creation—specifically, to guard it against the demonic. The baptism of the Holy Spirit expresses and empowers this entire universal commission.

In this life, then, our commission is to overwhelm the ruin of darkness and a broken covenant (see Deut. 28) with the forgiving, healing, restoring, demon-expelling, mighty power of God. The baptism of the Holy Spirit equips and empowers us to proclaim the Kingdom of God (ruling) over every life in the chaos of sin, sickness, and demonization and over every evil situation, to see it healed and redeemed for His glory.

Traditional theology is a "theology of preparation" ("repent and be baptized"), but it denies the very goal of this preparation—the charismatic Spirit. The New Testament, by contrast, sees the ideal as a single package—one's commission, which includes one's "calling," the *ordo salutis*, the baptism, and charismatic discipling of others.

The mission of Jesus is focused on developing the equipped, empowered disciple who, after *"he is fully trained will be* [exactly] *like His teacher"* (Luke 6:40 ESV). Paul demonstrated this principle in his explanation of discipleship: "Imitate me, exactly as I imitate Christ" (see 1 Cor. 11:1). Paul's Gospel was exactly like that of Jesus.[24] Jesus's earthly ministry ends with discipleship, not with the disciples going to Heaven. He explains their mission in this life as the same commission that God had always given to His children—"all authority" provided by the baptism of the Holy Spirit (see Matt. 28:19-20; Acts 1:8).

PART FOUR

EQUIPPING THE SAINTS

Dr. Randy Clark

Chapter 12

HOLINESS, SOCIAL JUSTICE, LEGALISM, AND BAPTISM IN THE HOLY SPIRIT

Any study of baptism in the Holy Spirit should include an emphasis on holiness because the ways in which holiness works itself out are worth consideration. There is a personal side of holiness, and there is a social side. One must ask, "What is the nature of holiness?" The danger is to move toward legalism and forget about the social dimension of holiness.

Legalism has diminished a lot since I became a minister 47 years ago. During the last half of the 19th century and the first half of the 20th century, other non-Pentecostal denominations were much more legalistic than they are today. The Holiness denominations, out of which Pentecostalism arose, were especially legalistic.

When I use the term *legalistic*, I am referring to rules of conduct typically applied to outward activities more than issues of the heart. Some of these rules that were (and to some extent are still) followed include the following: no smoking, no drinking, no card playing, no dancing, no going to the theater, no swimming with the opposite sex, no makeup for women, no long hair for men, no jewelry, no wearing of slacks for women, no short sleeves for men, and no owning of televisions. These cultural activities, among others, were seen as sin.

The danger with legalism is that it moves past the emphasis of Scripture, which doesn't have prohibitions on many of the things listed (of course some of them didn't exist in the biblical day), and it ignores Jesus's insight that it is not what goes into the mouth of a person that corrupts him but what comes out of the mouth that reveals the heart (see Matt. 15:17-18). Legalism surely adds a lot of new laws regarding the behavior of Christians that seem to violate the first council of the Church, as recorded in Acts 15, which dealt with the law and new believers.

I believe that Jesus related holiness to issues of the heart much more than to the rules of the "holy ones," or the Pharisees of His day. Today, once again, holiness must be refocused on the heart. After all, in response to the rich young ruler's question, *"Teacher, which is the greatest commandment in the Law?"* Jesus responds, *"'Love the Lord your God with all your heart and with all your soul and with all your mind.' This is the first and greatest commandment. And the second is like it: 'Love your neighbor as yourself.' All the Law and the Prophets hang on these two commandments"* (Matt. 22:36-40). Elsewhere Jesus similarly underscores the heart's centrality to holiness: *"A new command I give you: Love one another. As I have loved you, so you must love one another. By this all men will know that you are My disciples, if you love one another"* (John 13:34-35 NASB). And again, Jesus reveals what is really important in holiness in John 15, where He says, *"My command is this: Love each other as I have loved you"* and *"This is My command: Love each other"* (John 15:12,17).

The Apostle Paul also focuses the importance of love as a Christian virtue and sign of discipleship. He writes to the Romans, *"Let no debt remain outstanding, except the continuing debt to love one another, for he who loves his fellowman has fulfilled the law"* (Rom. 13:8). He continues, *"Love does no harm to its neighbor. Therefore love is the fulfillment of the law"* (Rom. 13:10).

Even when discussing spiritual gifts Paul keeps the focus on love as the motivation for the operation of the gifts. He writes to the Corinthians, *"Follow the way of love and eagerly desire spiritual gifts, especially prophecy"* (1 Cor. 14:1). First Corinthians 13, the great chapter on love, echoes this focus. By stressing the importance of love, Paul was not diminishing the significance of or limiting the gifts but rather emphasizing what he sees as their main inducement. I believe the gifts reveal the love of God to those who are touched by His gifts.

All of this is to say that Scripture places holiness in the context of love—loving God and loving people, especially those in the household of faith. This should determine how we exercise our freedom in grace. Once again, in his letter to the Galatians on Christian freedom in grace and the requirements of the law, Paul writes, *"For in Christ Jesus neither circumcision nor uncircumcision has any value. The only thing that counts is faith expressing itself through love"* (Gal. 5:6). A summation of the law is given again in Galatians 5:14: *"The entire law is summed up in a single command: 'Love your neighbor as yourself.'"*

This theme of love motivating the expression of the gifts is found elsewhere in the New Testament, from a variety of writers. The author of Hebrews asks us to *"consider how we may spur one another on toward love and good deeds"* (Heb. 10:24). James writes, *"If you really keep the royal law found in Scripture, 'Love your neighbor as yourself,' you are doing right"* (James 2:8). Peter similarly focuses on the importance of love, saying, *"Now that you have purified yourselves by obeying the truth so that you have sincere love for your brothers, love one another deeply, from the heart"* (1 Pet. 1:22). In First Peter he exhorts us: *"Above all, love each other deeply, because love covers over a multitude of sins"* (1 Pet. 4:8). In his first letter, the Apostle John comments, *"Whoever loves his brother lives in the light, and there is nothing in him to make him stumble"* (1 John 2:10). And in First John 3:11, he writes, *"This is the message you heard from the beginning: We should love one another,"* adding to this reminder by saying that *"we know that we have passed from death to life, because we love our brothers. Anyone who does not love remains in death"* (1 John 3:11,14). John has so many important references to love being indicative of truly belonging to God, especially in First John 4.

Clearly, the exercise of one's spiritual gifts inspired by the love of God is central in the life of the believer. But our understanding of who God is should not stop there. We must also realize that God is a God of justice and mercy and that these two aspects of His character are of major concern to Him. Scripture bears this out. There are 16 references to justice in the New Testament and 134 in the whole Bible. One of the most famous passages about justice and mercy is found in Micah 6:8: *"He has showed you, O man, what is good. And what does the Lord require of you? To act justly and to love mercy and to walk humbly with your God."*

Up until the 20th century, the revivals of past centuries had a social impact. This impact was not limited to a pietistic concern over personal sins; it also affected societal sins, mandating that the people of God act with justice and mercy on behalf of those who were being oppressed. In contrast, the revivals of the 20th century, particularly those after the 1920s, did not have as much of an impact on society, prompting one to ask why. I believe this shift in impact was the result of the Modernist-Fundamentalist Controversy in America. This controversy between liberals (modernists) and fundamentalists had been brewing for almost 100 years until it finally became a full-blown internal theological war. The liberals emphasized the social dimensions of the Gospel and the fundamentalists the personal. The two sides argued over who would have control over the denominational institutions, especially the colleges and the seminaries, with the liberals emerging victorious. With this split, the fundamentalists, who had most of the revivals, no longer focused on the social aspects of the Gospel.

This was a sad day indeed for the Church. This division, this rending asunder of the Gospel, should never have happened. I thank God that in the latter part of the 20th century and the beginning of the 21st century, these two parts of the Gospel have begun to be reunited. One of the greatest examples of such a reconciliation being effected is the work of Iris Global Ministries, the ministry of Drs. Rolland and Heidi Baker. Iris Global feeds the hungry, clothes the naked, drills water wells, provides education from elementary school through high school, and is presently building a Christian university that will be one of the best, if not the best, in the nation of Mozambique. In addition to all of this, they also heal the sick, preach the need for personal forgiveness of sins, cast out demons, and see people baptized in the Holy Spirit.

I believe in both the personal and the social aspects of the Gospel of the Kingdom. I believe in the need for people to be regenerated and filled with the Spirit, to be delivered from demonic influence, whether it is oppression or possession (possession can happen only to the lost, but degrees of being demonized can happen to the saved). I also believe that there is need for the powers and principalities of evil that become ingrained in the values, mores, and laws of societies to be challenged and overcome by the Church. These "philosophies of demons," like Nazism, Fascism, and Communism, which resulted in millions of lives lost, must be overcome and replaced by a system of law that is characterized by justice and mercy.[1] God is concerned about wages, working conditions, child labor, slavery, sex trafficking, boy soldiers, and all societal laws or practices that oppress people.

Perhaps W. J. Seymour, whom many believe should be called "the father of the Pentecostal movement," was right when, instead of seeing tongues as the initial sign of the baptism in the Holy Spirit, he saw the color line being washed away in the blood of Jesus as the evidence. This was in the day of Jim Crow laws, with their harsh enforcement of racial segregation. Yet because of the love of God that was touching the hearts of the people, at Azusa Street in California you could see black and white, Hispanic and Asian, all worshiping together without any sign of segregation. The implications of what God was doing at Azusa Street, with the outpouring of the Spirit, offered up the promise of massive impact for our nation. Had we been able to embrace fully this radical love, we might not have allowed racism and segregation to persist as long as they have in our country, nor economic injustice to prevail. But it is much easier to create rules of outward behavior and call them signs of holiness than it is to love as Jesus loved and as He told *us* to love. Love demands justice. Love demands mercy. Love demands care for the orphans and the widows. Love demands concern for the aliens within our borders. Love demands helping people escape from poverty.

How holiness that is connected to the baptism in the Holy Spirit is worked out in public policies and how social justice is reached bring us to the alternative approaches of both of our political platforms. I am old enough to remember the "Great Society" vision of President Lyndon B. Johnson. The beautiful apartments built in St. Louis to provide housing for the poor were torn down about 40 years later. They were a dangerous place in which to live. This social experiment on how to help the poor was motivated by a godly concern with a biblical basis, but it is clear that the response to these social ills did not work. We need wisdom from God on how to minister justice and mercy to the poor and needy without locking them into perpetual poverty. Revival has often brought such wisdom, as we shall see.

A few days ago I was in Brazil ministering in two large Baptist churches with several thousand in average attendance for each, and in a Presbyterian Charismatic church that had an average attendance of 7,000. I spoke in two other churches that had several thousand members each as well. While on this trip I spent time talking with the man whom God used to bring me into the things of the Spirit, Blaine Cook. While Blaine is an Associate Evangelist of Global Awakening, his full-time job is as a businessman. He has

one company that he started. But he is working on five other companies that have potential disruptive technologies. Blaine wants to
see these companies make a lot of money, and funnel back into the
communities money for social programs. Blaine is a great example of
a Christian whose life is so touched by the Holy Spirit that he wants
to, in tangible ways, reveal the love of God to the poor through both
social and personal aspects of the gospel. He told me he believes that
with every true revival there is a release of God's creativity resulting
in new technologies that are used to the betterment of humankind.
Blaine is an example of holiness without legalism that reveals the
heart of God for the oppressed and the poor.

Chapter 13

REVIVAL AND HOLY SPIRIT BAPTISM

*"Some talk as though the present age is not the
Holy Spirit's age. There is but one dispensation
of the Holy Spirit, and that one lies between
the first and second advents of our Lord."*[1]

—F. F. BOSWORTH (1877-1958)

In Hebrew, the word for *revive* is *chayah*, which means "to be quickened," "to be made alive," and "to be restored." Pentecost was the
first revival in the Church—the first time that the Church was
quickened and made alive, restoring the birthright of all believers.
Every genuine revival subsequent to Pentecost has been patterned
on that first event. At the first Pentecost, the Holy Spirit poured
Himself out, with salvations, miracles, signs, and wonders following,
and the number added to the Church greatly increased (in spite of
the naysayers and persecution). Is that not what happens today in
the midst of what we term "revival?" And for that matter, is that not
what has happened throughout the history of the Church whenever
there has been a mighty outpouring of God's Spirit on an individual
or a group of people? Is not corporate revival made up of personal

Pentecost—people touched by God's Spirit who then outwardly manifest this touch in their physical bodies and inwardly in spiritual formation and renewal that leads to Kingdom fruit?

When viewed thus, revival is a continuous event in the life of the Church, established for us by Jesus Christ as the impetus for the Great Commission. It is through His Spirit that God sustains His Bride. Those who are willing to give themselves fully to God in the power of His Spirit become pictures of the victorious Bride of Christ.

I believe the Church today is currently in a worldwide revival based on the number of churches being birthed, the vast number of people being saved, and the greatly increasing phenomenon of the outpouring of the gifts of the Holy Spirit such as signs, wonders, and people being raised from the dead. As has been true throughout the history of the Church, this current revival is not without controversy. My question to the Church is this: As we stand on the cusp of this great move of God's Spirit, will we be offended by new and novel manifestations of the baptism of the Holy Spirit, or will we remain open, observing and examining the fruit? I think we would do well to remember the following words of John Wesley: "Lord send us revival without its defects but if this is not possible, send revival, defects and all."[2]

Let the whole Body of Christ not tarry any longer in embracing our birthright. As Jon Ruthven said, we are God's servants, His true role models, whom He will always equip with the gift of being able to hear His voice, sense His presence, and to prophesy His love and authority over individuals and nations, experiencing the baptism in speech and power with the goal of discipling the nations.

While we can all hear from God, Holy Spirit baptism is not simply a matter of hearing and uttering God's word of power on occasions. Ideally, it should involve "walking in the Spirit" so that we are immersed and empowered on a continuing basis. When we walk in the Spirit in this manner we can experience the intense presence of Jesus, who will be with us *"to the end of the age"* (see Matt. 28:20).[3]

In the pages that follow we are going to take a cursory glance at revival in the last 300 years of the Protestant Church. I believe one definition of revival is "a special time in the Church when people are being empowered by the Spirit of God to have victory over besetting sins and habits, boldness to witness, and power to push back the kingdom of darkness through deliverance, healing, and the confrontation of philosophies of demons with the truth of God." This empowering experience is connected to being filled or baptized with the Holy Spirit. As you read through these historical accounts, it's difficult not to notice the pattern of Holy Spirit renewal and empowerment that runs throughout each one.

Great Awakenings

The First Great Awakening (1727–1750) brought great growth to the Church, both in England and its colonies. It is estimated that to reach the same number of people proportionately today, there would have to be two million saved in one year in America alone. Yet even in the midst of the significant growth of the First Great Awakening there was resistance. Wesley was locked out of the Anglican Church in York by one of its bishops, and both he and Whitefield were accused of fanaticism, emotionalism, and even of having powder up their sleeves that caused people to pass out.

The Second Great Awakening (1780–1810) began at Brown University at a time when America was deeply impacted by Deism. There were few Christians in any of the major universities of America at that time. Anti-Christian rioters were taking Bibles from pulpits and burning them in the streets.[4] Prior to this Second Great Awakening, few in America attended church with any regularity, and almost no new conversions were occurring. It was a low-water mark for the Church. A few souls at Brown University began crying out for revival, and God brought His fire. The spark that began at Brown

University soon spread to other colleges. Timothy Dwight, president of Yale University, had been touched in the First Great Awakening and was desperate for another move of God. At the time, there were almost no Christians at Yale University, which was a sad state of affairs for a school that had been established to train people for ministry. But God answered Timothy Dwight's prayers, and Yale was touched by the Second Great Awakening.[5]

The lawless frontier of the United States was the next place to see revival. It broke out in a little backwater town called Rogues' Harbor in Bourbon County, Kentucky, bringing hundreds of thousands into the Church. On the heels of the Rogues' Harbor revival came the great Cane Ridge revival that began in 1801. The spark that began among the Presbyterians spread to the Baptists and Methodists. The fruits of this revival saw in four years the Presbyterian Church in Kentucky double in size, while the Baptists tripled and the Methodists quadrupled.[6] It is interesting to note that the Methodists also had the greatest incidence of manifestations, to the point where these experiences were termed "Methodist fits." Cane Ridge was a high-water mark for the Second Great Awakening in the Church.

Within three years of Cane Ridge, one-third of the Christians in the South had experienced manifestations similar to what was observed at Cane Ridge. Many fell to the ground under the power of God, sometimes unable to get up or regain consciousness for hours or days at a time. Both believers and unbelievers alike were overcome with a jerking motion. Some of the jerking was so violent that bonnets flew from women's heads and combs came loose from their hair, letting their long braids flow. Sometimes the jerking was so pronounced it caused a whacking sound like that made by a whip. No one was safe from the influence of the Holy Spirit. Children would begin to preach in a manner that would otherwise have been impossible for them as they trembled, shook, laughed, barked, and became drunk in the Spirit. Interestingly, one of the greatest criticisms of the Toronto revival was the barking noises that some associated with it. I, as well as others who were in Toronto for many years, heard very few people actually barking. The fruits of Toronto have been enormous, but sadly many have not been able to see them because they have allowed the enemy to keep their gaze focused on what was most odd rather than what was most fruitful.

With all great revivals, there comes both praise and criticism that brings about change, and so it was with the Second Great Awakening. New denominations were created in the wake of the revival. The Presbyterian Church split into "New Lights" and "Old Lights," and the Cumberland Presbyterian denomination was formed. Peter Cartwright, a circuit-riding Methodist evangelist, was saved during this period, shortly after the Cane Ridge revival. Cartwright went on to become one of the greatest Methodist evangelists of his day. He saw manifestations similar to those at Cane Ridge in his meetings, with large numbers of people coming to Christ as a result of the power that accompanied his preaching of the Gospel. Dr. Elmer Towns, a Christian college professor and prolific author, has noted that the Second Great Awakening resulted in the abolition of slavery, the end of child labor, the beginning of the feminist movement, the move for universal literacy, and the reformation of the prisons.[7]

On the heels of the Second Great Awakening came the General Awakening (1825–1840). Finney and Edward Irving were instrumental in this move of God. Irving was a key figure in the origin of the Catholic Apostolic Church in London. Both would experience much criticism, not only for the manifestations in their meetings, but also for the doctrinal positions to which they adhered. In fact, Irving was defrocked for his kenotic understanding of the Incarnation. Finney was criticized for his Arminian views, but he would see over half a million people come to Christ.

In 1858, prayer revival began in Hamilton, Ontario, before spreading to New York City through businessman Jeremiah Lanphier, who called for noon-hour prayer meetings, causing revival to break out as thousands began to meet. Soon the flames burned from New York to the rest of the country. Between February and June 1858, 50,000 souls a week were being added to the Church, which had a population of 30 million in the United States. Meanwhile, across the pond, by 1865, a million souls had been saved in Great Britain, which had a population of roughly 27 million. But it didn't stop there. William Booth started the Salvation Army, Hudson Taylor began the China Inland Mission, and David Livingston and Mary Slessor focused attention on mission work in Africa, as the fruits of Holy Spirit baptism continued to fan the flames of revival.[8]

The Holiness-Pentecostal Revivals

Then came the Holiness-Pentecostal revivals (1875–1907), the Pentecostal revival reaching its height between 1901 and 1909. Typically, these two groups have not been associated with one another because the Pentecostal revival caused division among some of the 23 new denominations that formed in the United States between 1893 and 1900.[9] Yet both groups experienced similar phenomena: falling, shaking, trembling, roaring, crying, laughing, and drunkenness in the Holy Spirit. All of these were accompanied by visions, dreams, and experiences of empowerment that set people free from the grip of sin and brought sanctification. The Pentecostals added a new experience—speaking in tongues—as evidence of being baptized in the Holy Spirit. It was actually Charles Fox Parham who, in 1901 in Topeka, Kansas, would be the first to describe speaking in tongues as the initial evidence of baptism.

The dawn of the 20th century saw pockets of revival fire burning around the world. Thousands came to the Lord between 1902 and 1903 in Australia and New Zealand through the preaching of R. A. Torrey and Charlie Alexander. The great Welsh revival was birthed through young Evan Roberts when he received a mighty touch from God that brought empowerment for ministry. The Welsh revival was accompanied by all the usual manifestations seen in previous revivals and was instrumental in the start of numerous other revivals, particularly in the United States. Frank Bartleman, one of the early leaders in Pentecostalism in the United States, would communicate between the revival burning in Los Angeles and that of Evan Roberts in Wales revealing a close connection between the Holiness revival of 1904 and the Pentecostal revival of 1906.

Meanwhile, in 1905, revival broke out in a girl's orphanage in India that brought tongues, visions, raptures, and the infilling of the Holy Spirit. Upon hearing this news, the pastor of the Jotabeche Methodist Church in Santiago, Chile, became hungry for more of God. At the suggestion of one of his janitors, he called key leaders of the church to fasting and prayer for revival, and in short order the Spirit fell upon his church, resulting in tongues, prophecy, trembling, shaking, and falling, along with bold preaching in the streets of Santiago. Even though this pastor and his church were kicked out of his denomination, they would later become what was then the largest church in the world.[10]

In 1906, the Azusa Street revival broke out in Los Angeles under the leadership of Seymour, causing the hot spot of revival to move from Wales to Los Angeles. People came from all over the world to receive and then carry the Pentecostal message and experience back home. Thousands were baptized in the Holy Spirit, spreading the fires of revival via Pentecostalism to Europe. All of this was not without controversy. New leaders of the nascent Pentecostal Church of the Nazarene would reject Azusa Street and its message of tongues as the necessary and initial sign of the baptism in the Spirit, even removing the word "Pentecostal" from its name. Some early Pentecostal preachers were chased out of towns, while others were tarred and feathered. Yet God's purposes would not be thwarted. As many as tried to put out the fire of the Spirit, greater numbers caught the flame. In 1907, revival broke out in Pyongyang, in what is now North Korea, eventually giving rise to David Yonggi Cho's church of over 800,000 members in Seoul, South Korea.

Some view all of these mighty moves of God as multiple revivals, but I see them as evidence of one great worldwide move of God that has not abated. Although revival tends to wax and wane, God continues to spread the baptism of His Holy Spirit across the face of the globe. I also believe our expectation that revivals need to last about three years should be scrapped. Many of the great revivals in history lasted for 20 to 50 years.

Mid-20th Century Revivals

In the middle of the 20th century, another great move of God arose out of the Pentecostal movement that spread around the world and renewed a great missionary movement. There were three different streams that contributed to this revival. One was the Latter Rain movement, which emerged out of Saskatchewan, Canada, in 1947 and involved the teaching and practice of prophetic presbyteries for the impartation of gifts of the Holy Spirit as well as the confirmation of people in their positions in the local church and in the mission field. This, along with the teaching regarding the manifest sons of God, caused great controversy.

Not everyone rejected the Latter Rain movement, though. The Elim Pentecostal denomination instead worked to correct some of its excesses and unorthodox teachings. One of my favorite testimonies comes from a former president of Elim College. He tells of a man sent to Kenya out of a prophetic presbytery during the Latter Rain movement. After several months of not leading anyone to Jesus, this missionary cried out to the Lord, asking why he had moved his entire family to Kenya, believing it was the will of God, only to see nothing happen. Not long after this prayer, he was standing on the street when a funeral procession began to pass by. The casket was being carried on the shoulders of several men. As he stood there watching, the Lord spoke to him, telling him to go and lay hands on the casket and command the man inside to be raised to life. Believing he had heard from God, he obeyed. As he carried out this directive, the people heard the dead man knocking on the inside of the casket. He was raised, and as a result of this miracle, a revival broke out that led to the birth of over 10,000 churches.

I spoke with two leaders (who are now in their 70s and 80s), one who had been involved in the 1947 Latter Rain revival from the beginning and another who had participated in the 1948 healing revival. In the course of our conversation, they shared their thoughts on why each revival had eventually waned. The pastor who had been involved in the 1948 healing revival said this to me: "There were so many healings that they began to be taken for granted, and the people lost the ability to be awed by what God was doing. This grieved the heart of God."

The minister from the 1947 Latter Rain revival told me the following: "I was in a meeting in Detroit one night when I heard the Spirit say, 'I was pouring out My Spirit on apostles, prophets, evangelists, pastors, and teachers in order to equip the saints, but you have focused on the office and who has the office rather than doing what the office was created to do—equip the saints. For this reason, I am lifting My Spirit, and it will not return for…'"—I forgot the specific number of years, but it was about the time of the beginning of the Charismatic Renewal.

Then he went on to say, "There were a lot of things men said [that] were wrong with the revival, and I am sure there were some excesses somewhere, but these were not the norm; and what our critics said about us wasn't what the Lord was concerned about. He was concerned about 'equipping the saints' or, more exactly, our failure to equip the saints. This was God's big issue with the Latter Rain movement."

This period of revival was not just experienced among Pentecostals. In 1949, before he was well known, Billy Graham had an encounter with the Holy Spirit while in the mountains of Southern California at the Forest Home retreat center as he poured out his heart's desire for more of God. Shortly thereafter, his ministry took off, and he became known throughout the United States and eventually around the world, illustrating that revival isn't just for the Pentecostals. God has always been reaching out to His whole Church, to all who would have an eye to see and an ear to listen.

During this same year, evangelist Duncan Campbell would be used of God for a great revival in the Hebrides Island of Lewis off the coast of Scotland. This revival seems to have been prayed in by two elderly sisters. Accounts indicate that Duncan's role as evangelist was connected to their prayers as well. I mention this in part because many of the great moves of God have been preceded by times of intense prayer, but that is the subject for another study.

In 1952, a revival broke out on the campus of Asbury College (now University) that shook this Methodist Holiness institution. Public confession of sin, weeping, and repentance were hallmarks of this move of God. Asbury College would experience another revival in 1970 that was again characterized by public confession of sin, weeping, and evangelism.

On Easter Sunday, 1960, Episcopal priest Dennis Bennett shocked the Protestant Church when he announced from the pulpit that he had been baptized in the Holy Spirit with evidence of tongues. The religious establishment responded with equal measures of shock, alarm, and excitement, but one thing was for certain: the "underground" Pentecostal movement was no longer underground, nor was it confined to Pentecostals. Bennett's Holy Spirit baptism launched the Catholic Charismatic Renewal and would over time lead to the explosive growth of Charismatic Christianity. A Pew study completed in 2011 revealed there were over 300 million Charismatic Christians in the world. These 300 million comprised 14 percent of those who self-identified as Christians in the world at the time of the study. This number does not include the Pentecostals that represented 25 percent of the Christians in the world at that time. Between these two groups, nearly 40 percent of the Christians in the world are Pentecostal/Charismatic, and they are the fastest growing segment of the Church.[11]

The next wave of revival to sweep through the Church was the Jesus movement, which began around 1968 in the midst of the Charismatic movement. It began with God touching hippies and then branched out into the larger culture while remaining focused on young people. Millions of teens and those in their early 20s were saved through the Jesus movement—and not just in the United States, but around the world as well. The Jesus movement peaked around 1972. My class at The Southern Baptist Theological Seminary was the largest to date due to the Jesus movement. Like many moves of God, there were both controversies and fruits.

About this time, there occurred a great Indonesian revival, which was chronicled by Mel Tari in his book *Like a Mighty Wind*. Tari's book was popular but controversial due to the extraordinary supernatural miracles to which he testified. Because of their extraordinary nature, some insisted the stories were exaggerations. Rolland Baker (of Iris Global), a close friend of Tari's who had Mel as his best man in his wedding, says that the events in Tari's book not only are true, but that Mel only shared the "tamer" miracles and events because he knew the Western mind would have trouble believing what God did in Indonesia.

The Third Wave Revival

The Third Wave revival (1982–1986) was led by John Wimber and the Vineyard movement, but there were others who were also involved. These "others" were people who identified as Evangelicals but who embraced the operation of all the gifts for the Church today. They believed a person could be baptized in the Holy Spirit after conversion and sometimes at conversion, though this was less true experientially. They also believed in speaking in tongues, and they thought that tongues could occur before, at the moment of, or after the baptism in the Spirit.

The Third Wave revival was controversial because it was neither classical Pentecostal nor Evangelical in theology regarding the gifts and the baptism in the Spirit.[12] Controversy also arose over its contemporary music and the manifestations of the Spirit, which were primarily shaking, trembling, and falling under the power of God. The Association of Vineyard Churches grew to over several hundred in just a few years. This number does not include the other movements not associated with Vineyard churches.

Revival in the Last Decade of the 20th Century

The mid 1990s witnessed the beginnings of yet another revival. This particular move of God has been called by many names: "the Laughing revival," "the Toronto Blessing," "the Brownsville revival," and "the Smithton Awakening." It began in 1992 in Argentina, with pastor Claudio Freidzon. Miracles, signs, and wonders broke out in his church, followed by explosive growth. On the heels of this Holy Spirit fire in Argentina, "fire" broke out in Lakeland, Florida, at Karl Strader's church, the Carpenter's Home Church. This happened when the evangelist Rodney Howard-Browne came to speak. People fell down under the power of God, oftentimes unable to get up for quite some time. Weeping and laughter also characterized this particular move of God. Many considered the laughter a new and novel manifestation when in fact laughter can be found during other outpourings, within both Protestant and Roman Catholic revival history.

Then, in January 1994, revival broke out in Toronto, Canada, when I went to speak for a planned four-day meeting. I was the bridge between Howard-Browne and what happened in Toronto. I had gone to receive ministry from Rodney twice before going to Toronto. The outpouring of the Spirit happened in my church for months and at the regional meeting of the Vineyard in the Midwest when I spoke. This revival in Toronto became the longest protracted meeting in Western history, with people gathering six nights a week for twelve and a half years until the summer of 2006. The influence from Toronto quickly spread around the world. During the first two years, over two million people came to Toronto for the meetings. Some say as many as four million came during the first five years, and reports indicate over 50,000 churches were touched during the first three to four years. An army of itinerates who had been touched by God went out to preach the Good News. It would not be an exaggeration to believe that thousands went out to the nations. The controversy over Toronto was great, just as it was during the First Great Awakening, the Second Great Awakening, the Holiness revival, the Pentecostal revival, the mid-20th-century revival, the Charismatic Renewal, and the Third Wave revival. However, I can testify to the authenticity of this move of God because He birthed it through me. I wrote the book *There Is More*[13] to reveal the massive good fruit of this move and to provide a biblical and historical basis for the doctrine of laying on of hands (see Heb. 6:1-2). Previous to this I had written a book called *Lighting Fires*[14] that describes how this move came about.

It is impossible to know how many souls have come into the Kingdom as a result of God's touch in Toronto, but I do know with certainty that the testimony of three people in particular who were profoundly touched by God in Toronto has been used to lead over a million to the Lord. They are Henry Madava (Ukraine), Heidi Baker (Mozambique), and Leif Hetland (Pakistan). This number does not include the thousands saved in Brazil as a result of the Toronto revival. Neither does it include the evangelistic fruit of the continued ministry of Howard-Browne, nor that of the Brownsville/Pensacola revival or the Smithton revival. I can only speak personally to some of the fruit I am aware of that is related to what happened in and through those who were impacted by the outpouring of the Spirit in Toronto.

The next outbreak of revival occurred on Father's Day, 1995, in Brownsville and Pensacola, Florida, and continued into 2000. Steve Hill was the evangelist, and John Kilpatrick was the pastor. Large numbers of people attended (I am not sure how many, but I would guess hundreds of thousands to millions), and many who were there went into the ministry, preaching the Gospel around the world. In 1996, pastor Steve Gray experienced revival in his church in Smithton, Missouri—a church that was literally in a cornfield. Thousands came, and lives were radically changed. These meetings, in which attendees experienced manifestations such as laughing, falling, being stuck to the floor, and being thrown backwards, continued for several years. As usual, with the manifestations came controversies.

One Mighty Move of God

I believe these revivals that occurred during the last decade of the 20th century were not, in actuality, multiple revivals, but rather were one mighty move of God. In a similar way, the Great Evangelical Revival in England and the First Great Awakening in America were both part of one major move of God. The same is true for the Second Great Awakening that broke out throughout the United States and for the mid-19th-century revivals in America, England, Scotland, the Hebrides Island of Lewis, and other locations. The great Holiness-Pentecostal revival that began near the end of the 19th century and continued into the first decade of the 20th century occurred simultaneously in several countries and continents at the same time, as did the revivals in 1947, 1948, 1949, and 1952. None of these were scattered revivals, in my opinion, but were expressions of one mighty move of God during that time.

Bill Johnson has shared on many occasions his story of a God encounter that profoundly changed his life. Bill is a fifth-generation pastor whose family has a rich history with the Lord. One night, many years after his initial baptism in the Holy Spirit, Bill was awakened by forceful spasms racking his body. He had been pressing in for more of the presence of God in his life for many months, and now God's manifest presence was on him and it wasn't pretty. He had absolutely no control over his body. As he lay there in the dark, contemplating what it would mean for his life and ministry if he remained a spastic permanently, he began to realize that the presence of God meant more to him than ministry, more than life itself. "If remaining a spastic means that I can remain in Your presence," said Bill, "then so be it." Into the night he lay there with his body out of control, until gradually the spasms ceased. The experience of God's presence and power lasted for hours, and it continued over the course of the next few nights, again waking him from his sleep. Bill continues to contend for more of God's presence, even if it means giving up everything. He has found the Pearl of Great Price and will not let go.

Two thousand years ago, a handful of men gave their lives for the spread of the Gospel. They walked and lived beside God in the flesh, and when He sent His precious Holy Spirit, they received it without hesitation. On the Day of Pentecost, after the Holy Spirit had fallen on those assembled, *"some made fun of them and said, 'They have had too much wine.' Then Peter stood up with the Eleven, raised his voice and addressed the crowd: '...In the last days, God says, I will pour out My Spirit on all people...I will show wonders in the heaven above and signs on the earth below"* (Acts 2:13,14,17,19). A little later, after the healing of the crippled beggar, Peter again addresses the naysayers: *"the God of Abraham, Isaac and Jacob, the God of our fathers, has glorified His servant Jesus,"* said Peter. *"Repent, then, and turn to God, so that your sins may be wiped out, that times of refreshing may come from the Lord, and that He may send the Christ, who has been appointed for you—even Jesus"* (Acts 3:13,19-20).

The time of God's refreshing is always available to us. How are we to receive such a great gift as the Holy Spirit when He comes to us? Just as Jesus did—with prayer and thanksgiving for every opportunity to give glory to God. Imagine the Church fully embracing the presence and power of God. Nothing could contain such an explosive power of Heaven. Without God's power working within us, we are always and everywhere out of our spiritual depth. But with Him, all things are possible. The good people of God whom I have labored beside for many years in ministry are not extremists. While they may often seek the extreme presence of God, they seek it from a place of balance and spiritual maturity. They are willing to risk it all for Jesus because they know Him intimately. Rather than fearing His presence and power, they earnestly desire these things for the work of ministry. They are willing to fall down, shake, roll, weep, and cry out for God if it means getting up with a greater capacity to love like Jesus and the power to resist sin in their lives. They are possessed with an unquenchable hunger and thirst for more of God. They run toward the source of the power of the risen Jesus Christ so that they may know Him better and make Him known. They seek the Giver, not the gifts, and above all else, they seek His heart of love.

As we stand on the edge of God's revival fire burning around the world in the 21st century, will we continue to be offended when God shows up in ways that confound our natural minds, or will we be courageous enough to reach out and take hold of our birthright as believers? Will we remain open to observe and examine the fruit, as Jonathan Edwards recommended? I encourage you to seek Him and let His love overtake you; then watch where it takes you.

Let us consider those who sought Him, whose lives were overtaken by His love, and where it took them.

Chapter 14

My Personal Testimonies and Others' Testimonies of Holy Spirit Baptism

I want to conclude this study of the baptism of the Holy Spirit with my own four testimonies of being filled or baptized with the Holy Spirit. I hope that by the time you read this I can say "five testimonies" because I am hungry for a fresh touch, a fresh filling, a fresh baptism.

My first baptism in the Holy Spirit occurred at the Baptist church I was pastoring in Spillertown, Illinois. I was 32 years old. I had already received my personal prayer language or "tongues" at the age of 19. I never considered this experience at 19 as my baptism in the Holy Spirit. There was too little power associated with it and too little new fruit for me to consider it a Spirit baptism. However, things were different with the experience of the Spirit when I was 32. This second experience was powerful, and it produced new fruit. "Fruit," as used by Jesus in John 15, is the fruit of doing rather than the fruit of being, to which Paul refers in Galatians 5:22. This new fruit first became apparent when I prayed for people and they fell down under the power of God. Also, I was now flowing in words of knowledge and seeing more people get healed in a month than

I had seen in the 14 years combined prior to this baptism/filling of the Spirit.

What did this experience look like or feel like for me? I began to shake from the power in my hands. The electricity was so strong that it coursed through my entire body. So much electricity went through me that it had the same effect as walking into an electric fence on a farm. These fences on farms have enough electricity to keep a horse, cow, or hog from going through them. The electric jolt hurts! I accidently stepped into them several times as a teenager. For hours afterward, the joints in my body would ache.

The day after I experienced God's empowering presence, all my joints ached as if I had walked into an electric fence. In addition to feeling electricity, I felt this presence, this power, touching me. It was like someone was gently pushing me. I didn't know what to do so I resisted it, thinking I was to do all I could to remain standing. I wasn't knocked off my feet, but if I hadn't moved my feet and tightened up my muscles to keep standing, I would have fallen. This force, this power, created the sensation that I was being pushed forward instead of backward, although many people feel they are being pushed backward when they encounter the power of God.

Five years later, I received my second filling or baptism in the Holy Spirit. This experience was physically more powerful; however, not as much new fruit came from it. I did receive greater clarity about the call on my life, though at the time I was unable to receive the prophecy connected with this filling/baptism in the Spirit—it was just too grandiose for my mind. One significant personal fruit was the power to overcome a demonic stronghold in my life with which I had been struggling. After this experience I became the victor instead of the victim. I experienced a sovereign deliverance without anyone even saying, "Come out!"

This second baptism occurred in October 1989, and it was more powerful than my conversion, as far as the manifesting presence of God. I received this fresh baptism during a regional meeting for the

Association of Vineyard Churches. The last night of the meeting, Todd Hunter was speaking on "Obedience," and near the end of his message, I felt the Holy Spirit affect me. I had hot tears running down my face—tears of confirmation and God's heart for evangelism. I had a strong impression of a five-fold ministry with evangelism as my calling. I heard, "You're for evangelism—you have always loved leading people to the Lord and preaching evangelistically."

I went forward and the regional overseer, Happy Leman, came to me and prayed for me. Then I felt I needed to have Steve Nicholson pray for me. He did, and he asked God for His purpose to be renewed in me. I could hardly keep standing, and the power in my hands intensified. They were shaking from the electricity coursing through them. I stayed at the front for about ten minutes because I could feel God's presence. As I turned to leave, Ron Allen, another regional overseer, from another region, came up to me and said, "The enemy has tried to take your son, but he did not succeed. Joshua and you will stand hand in hand before the nations. He will not ride your coattails; you will ride His because His anointing will eclipse yours." Ron left, and I sat to write down what he had told me. When I did, I began to weep.

I went to Ron to ask him about evangelism, and when I did, he said that what I was sensing was true. Ron then prayed for me, and when he prayed, there was a strong anointing. My chest shook, and I could feel electricity channeling into my chest from his hand. My right hand began to feel electricity and to shake. I heard someone blow on my chest, and at that moment I was "slain in the Spirit." It was as if I had been pushed down. Unlike my first baptism, I could not resist the power and remain standing.

I fell to the floor and everything intensified. I wept uncontrollably and prayed, "Thank You, God." The power began to strengthen and intensify. In addition to experiencing power, I felt this tremendous heat—so much heat that I began to sweat profusely. This was a supernatural heat because the room was air-conditioned and no one else was sweating. I have seen this tremendous heat happen to others about four to five times in my 47 years of ministry. The power became so painful that I heard myself cry out, "O God!" My hands were becoming contorted, and I could not unlock my fingers. At the same time, my face felt like electrical power was coursing through it, and I was experiencing a weight upon my chest that felt like an electric vise grip. My arms were pulled up over my head and my body stretched. My feet began cramping. The power would intensify each time Ron prayed over me for "evangelism."

Finally, after about 45 minutes the sensations began to leave and my breathing slowed. I became very aware of everything that was happening and began sobbing. I had no fear through it all, just love from God. I got up and was still somewhat weak. For over an hour I had to keep my hands above my belt because if I didn't, the electricity would become so strong in them that they would hurt. I felt this was a confirmation from God that I was to evangelize in my church and beyond. Looking back, I realize that years after this event, I had another insight, one I hadn't considered the day after the baptism occurred. The prophecy Ron gave me was about my son and myself. He said, "When you are older, you will travel the nations." Now I realize this experience was not just for evangelism, for it also would be preparatory for the ministry of impartation and healing in which I would be involved within four years of this baptism.

There would be another two impartations/fillings/baptisms to follow. In the summer of 1993, Rodney Howard-Browne would be used of God to lay hands on me. When he did, I fell to the ground but did not experience electricity, pain, energy, or heat. All I felt was tremendous peace, which God knew I needed. At the time, I was on the verge of a nervous breakdown from the pressure of pastoring the church that my wife, DeAnne, and I had started eight years earlier. The next day, I got in line again five times to receive prayer! I fell down under the power of God every time but never felt anything but peace and a weightiness that made it difficult to rise from the floor. When I flew home, I was not confident that anything of significance had happened to me because this experience was much less dramatic and powerful than the baptisms I had received in 1984 and 1989. How wrong I was!

The next day was Sunday, and for the first time in the St. Louis Vineyard church the power of God came with such force that people fell to the floor. I had prayed for people in other churches who had fallen but never anyone in the St. Louis Vineyard. Heaven broke loose that morning in the 8:30 A.M. service. Some of the people who fell under the power couldn't get off the floor until 4:30 that afternoon. People were filled, healed, and delivered. This continued, although not as intensely, almost every Sunday that I was at the church for the next eight years. It was common for people to fall under the power during the Sunday service. I have written about these experiences in greater detail in my book *Lighting Fires*.

In October 1993, just a few weeks after the experience in Tulsa when Rodney Howard-Browne prayed for me, I spoke at the Midwest Regional Vineyard Conference. This conference was for the pastors and their spouses from the region. Once again, the power of God fell upon the meeting. Every person there except one (there were about 80 people present) was touched by the Holy Spirit. There was great joy, laughing, crying—feeling bathed in God's love—people falling to the floor, sometimes multiple times, under His power; sovereign inner healings; and sovereign physical healings—healings by God that occurred without anyone ministering to the person. The people were deeply encouraged and strengthened by this visitation.

At the National Board and Council meeting of key Vineyard leaders a few weeks later, Happy Leman shared what had happened at the Midwest Regional Vineyard Conference. John Arnott, at the time an area overseer in Toronto in the Association of Vineyard Churches, was desperate to experience more of God. He and his wife, Carol had been spending their mornings in prayer and worship, asking for more of God for over six months. He had recently been to Argentina, where he was ministered to by Claudio Freidzon. A similar move of the Spirit, with much joy and laughter, had been happening there since 1992.

Upon hearing Happy's testimony, John called me and asked if I would come to Toronto. I told him I would but said that what had happened at the Midwest Regional meeting might never happen again. John still insisted that I come, and so I agreed to come for four days. I had only one testimony and one sermon worth preaching so I decided to bring my children's pastor, Bill Mares, who had been with me at the meeting in August with Rodney Howard-Browne. I would preach twice to the adults, and Bill would preach once to the children and once to the teenagers; then we would go home. I also took my worship leader and his wife, Gary and Anni Shelton, and my son Josh.

I was so nervous that God wasn't going to use me in Toronto that I drove from St. Louis to Lakeland, Florida, to listen to Rodney Howard-Browne one more time. I was hoping that he might have an opportunity to pray for me again. I wanted a fresh touch of the Holy Spirit—more anointing for Toronto. In Lakeland, Rodney noticed the Spirit of God touching me. He called me out and prayed for me, and I fell to the floor. However, this time I didn't sense the weight on me. I felt like I could get up, yet I didn't try. Instead, I said, "Lord, You are not my cosmic bell-hop. You are not my servant; I am Your servant. I am going to wait on You to come and touch me. I am going to lay here waiting until You come touch me, or until the janitor makes me get up." After several minutes I began to feel eletricity in my hands, much as I had in 1989. But this time the sensation was even more intense. I looked at my hands. My fingers were being pulled down toward my palms, my knuckles were locked, and my hands were very cold. They became rigid, and I couldn't move my fingers. When Rodney saw what was happening, he came to me, looked up to the several thousand onlookers, and said, "This is the power of God in your hands. Go home and pray for everyone in your church."

The following Sunday, at the end of the service, I told my congregation that I was going to dismiss them and that they could go, but if they would like to be prayed for, they should stay and I would pray for them. Almost everyone stayed and about 90 percent of those I prayed for fell to the floor under the power of God.

Even after this, my faith was weak that God would use me in Toronto. Yet God, in His goodness and mercy, used a prophecy to radically build a strong faith in me that He *was* in fact going to use me in Toronto. The prophecy came through Richard Holcomb, a friend I had met in Texas. Twice God had Richard call me and give me prophetic words, yet I could not believe them. I thought Richard was wrong when he called me the first time and told me he saw hundreds of thousands of lights that represented people and that I would preach to crowds of 100,000 and be used in revival. Then, he called me another time and told me of a dream he had in which he saw that a great dam had broken and the floodwaters were hitting a town in front of it. He said he believed this dream represented a great revival that was coming and that I would be a key leader in this revival. At the time, I didn't have 50 people in our new church plant so I found it hard to believe either of these words. I said to my wife, DeAnne, "Richard is telling me that I will speak to 100,000 people. I would just like to speak to 100!"

But then, right before I was set to go to Tornoto, Richard called with another word for me, and this time I believed him because of the timing. It was ten o'clock at night, the night before I was to leave for Toronto. I was very nervous and anxious that God would not use me. Richard called, not knowing I was leaving in a few hours. When I answered the phone, he said, "Randy, I have the second clearest word I have ever had for you. The Lord says, 'Test Me now. Test Me now. Test Me now. Do not be afraid—I will back you up. Like Elijah prayed for Gehazi's eyes, I want your eyes to be open to see My resources for you in the heavenlies. And do not become anxious, because when you become anxious, you can't hear Me.'" I knew in my heart that his word was from God. It took all my fear away and gave me great boldness. Because of this word, I was able to go to Toronto expecting great things to happen—but not nearly as great as they actually were!

Now, 23 years after that initial visit to Toronto, where I had planned to speak twice over a period of four days because I only had two sermons worth preaching, literally over three million people have been saved through just three people over whom I prayed. In addition, more than a million have been saved through others I've prayed for, or through someone God touched through my ministry. And scores of thousands of churches have been started. Those initial four meetings were extended, continuing six nights a week for twelve and a half years. I have continued to fulfill the prophetic words given from 1984 until 1994—that I would go to the nations and that God was going to use me to lay hands on pastors and leaders to be activated in the Holy Spirit and have gifts imparted to them. For 23 years I have traveled throughout the world, preaching on healing and activation through impartation. I have seen the effects of power evangelism as I have watched the power of God heal and soften the hearts of the lost, helping them see the compassion of God in a tangible way, as well as His nearness. But, the fruit of these impartations wasn't only for power to minister. I also received power to live a more holy life, having greater victory over sin than prior to the experience of God's power.

When I met Dr. Vinson Synan at Regent University in 1995, he asked if I had a Holiness background. "No," I replied. "I was raised and trained as a Baptist." With that, he proceeded to tell me that my testimony of the baptism of the Spirit in 1989 liberating me from sin was one of the most powerful testimonies of holiness he had heard in a long time. He realized that I didn't have a doctrine regarding holiness but that I did have an experience.

The baptisms in the Holy Spirit that I have received have released in me gifts of the Holy Spirit that I was not moving in prior to these touches from God—gifts of boldness and faith for witness, freedom over sin, and preparation for a new role and calling on my life. In thinking back to what was going on in my life before these four baptisms—March 1984, October 1989, August 1993, and January 1994—I realize that I had become very desperate for more of God. This desperation resulted in fasting and prayer for more—to be filled or baptized in the Spirit. I had fasted for two weeks before the first filling-baptism in March 1984. And I had been fasting for two weeks before the impartation in Tulsa in August 1993, and again for two weeks before the filling-baptism-impartation in Lakeland, where I experienced God's empowering presence in January 1994, just two weeks before going to Toronto. I not only sought God through fasting, but I was willing to go hear ministers whom I believed carried an anointing for impartation: John Wimber in January 1984 and Rodney Howard-Browne in 1993 and 1994. I also reached out to invite people to come to my church who could bring their gift for impartation to my church—namely, Blaine Cook in March 1984. In addition to fasting, I sought God in prayer. I prayed on my knees to be a coin in God's pocket, telling Him that He could spend me any way He wanted. I told God that if He would touch me, just one more time, that I would go anywhere and do anything He told me. I read many biographies and books on the Holy Spirit, His gifts, and His baptism-filling-impartation, and listened to many teachings. All this is to say that I have been hungry for more of God, and He has responded to my hunger. And I believe He will do the same for you.

Other Testimonies

As this book came together, I realized that not all the testimonies of Holy Spirit baptism of which I know could be included. That being said, I have included four more firsthand testimonies that are significant because I believe they illustrate yet again the great diversity of experience that is inherent in the baptism of the Holy Spirit. In each of these testimonies, I see one or more of the three prerequisites that indicate to me the authenticity of the experience: a personal awareness of the inadequacy of one's Christian life, a desire for one's personal condition to change that manifests in a profound hunger to be a victorious Christian, and a desire that one's life honors God through service that brings Him glory. The fourth testimony is also proof that God can and will touch us even under the most unexpected and unusual circumstances.

Rex Burgher

"If you are dry and thirsty and need a fresh touch from God, come forward." Such was the altar call from John Wimber. Within minutes, our family was at the front with close to 1,000 other people. We stood, extending our hands out in front of us, as we quieted our hearts and waited on God. It was May 1995, and we were unaware that the fire of revival that God had sparked through Randy Clark in 1994 in Toronto had spread to Kelowna, British Columbia, where we were attending a conference with Wes Campbell. Nor did we realize the impact of what God was about to do on our lives. What happened to us that day changed everything for us and for many others, I believe, for generations to come.

I had no paradigm for what happened next to me. I fell. I don't know why I fell; I had never fallen before, nor had I ever felt like I would fall over when receiving prayer. But that day in Kelowna I fell. Now I understand that we fall because we can't stand when the presence and power of God comes upon us, but back then I didn't know what was happening to me.

Lying there on the floor, I didn't have angelic visitations or visions. No Scriptures began to pour into my mind. I didn't have any indication that something was happening to me. I just felt peace. I felt complete peace about lying there. I wasn't worried about myself or those around me. When I finally got up from the floor, I was instantly aware of a tremendous, overwhelming transformation that was taking place within me. In the few seconds that it took for me to get to my feet, I felt like I had entered into a different realm of reality. The change was startling. It was as if I was submerged in a pool of water. I felt like I was underwater with my eyes open, moving in slow motion. I was overwhelmed and in shock, but at the same time I felt enveloped in an incredible peace.

As I stood there with the glory of God resting upon me, I tried to speak, and as I did, something began to come out from the depths of my belly. I felt a rushing, gurgling brook of power that began to bubble up from my belly and out through my lips. No words would come forth—just a bubbling, gurgling brook. Later, I was able to describe it as similar to the experience of turning on a garden hose that has been lying in the hot sun and has developed pockets of water and air. When the water begins to move down the hose, it pushes those pockets of air and water along, creating spurts of water, then air, then water, then air, until finally all the air has been pushed out and the water can flow freely. I felt as if air and water were coming out me. I could actually feel and see the moisture. Moist air would come out of my mouth when I tried to speak.

Whenever I tried to communicate with people near me, they would immediately collapse onto the floor. At one point I decided to try a different approach. I went up to someone without trying to speak to him, but the result was the same—he immediately fell to the floor. Normally all of this would have been quite alarming, but I wasn't the least bit alarmed because of the overwhelming peace of God that enveloped me. With this peace of the Lord upon me, I began to approach people whose backs were turned to me, but as I came up behind them and raised my hand to tap them on the shoulder, they would collapse before I could even touch them. Within a few minutes, anyone who was within a 20-foot radius of me was on the floor, under the power of God.

After this encounter with God, Lois and I were never the same. We would fall asleep at night, only to be awakened as our bodies would begin to tremble and shake under His anointing and power. At times, the most gentle nudging of the Holy Spirit would wake one or the other of us out of a deep sleep, causing us to whisper the holy name of Jesus, and then the trembling and shaking would begin. If either of us were asleep, we would wake the other up because the shaking was so uncontrollable. This went on for hours every night for six months, as wave after wave of the Holy Spirit swept over us. We began to wonder if we would ever sleep through the night again. Then we began to notice that it didn't matter if we were awake or asleep. We were experiencing God's tangible presence continually—and sometimes in the strangest of places. We had become carriers of the anointing, and wherever we went, the fire of God manifested itself upon the people with whom we came into contact.

When we returned home, on our first Sunday back at church, which was Pentecost Sunday, 1995, our pastor asked us to come forward and pray for people. When we did, the fire fell, changing the direction and focus of the church for years to come. So dramatic was the impact of God's visitation upon our church that we ended up setting aside one night of each week as "Renewal Night." For over a year, thousands of people came to receive a fresh touch of God's presence.

The more Lois and I and our family sought God, the more doors began to open for us to travel and spread the fire of a fresh baptism of His love. In March 1999, we met Randy Clark on our first ministry trip to Brazil with Global Awakening. Within a month of that trip, Randy had asked if we would consider moving to St. Louis to work with him. We felt it was the Lord's call, and so we moved to St. Louis where we entered into a time of intense ministry, traveling the world with Randy. For three years, Lois and I worked alongside Randy until we felt the Lord calling us to begin our own ministry. Since that time, we have ministered in over 19 countries.

We have seen thousands saved, healed, and delivered, and we continue to spread the love of God to all we meet. The fire of revival has not waned in our lives, and the supernatural anointing power to touch individuals and churches has not diminished as we continue to spread the fire. In the midst of the process, God has taught us what it means to live and walk in holiness, giving us victory over personal issues as He molds and shapes us into ones who never stop hungering and thirsting to know more our Father in Heaven.[1]

Ben Scofield

I think that to properly understand the context of the baptism of the Holy Spirit in my life it's best to start with how I received an impartation for healing and words of knowledge before the baptism of the Holy Spirit. Until the age of 18, I was essentially backslidden, or at best lukewarm, although I'm not sure there is a difference.

When my family moved back to the United States from the missions field, I had an encounter with the Lord and gave my life to Him. Within a few months, I was attending a church in St. Louis, Missouri, one that had hosted Randy Clark for a series of meetings. Because I wanted to be used by God and was trying to be actively involved in the church, I decided to sign up to be on the ministry team, where I received training from Randy's team. During this time I did not have a major encounter with the Holy Spirit. Then, on the night that Randy taught on words of knowledge followed by impartation, I began to operate both in words of knowledge and in healing on a level I had never experienced before. What followed was an amazing whirlwind period of two years of ministry alongside Randy.

The words of knowledge and ministry of healing increased gradually as I ministered with Randy over the next couple of years. At one point, I spent several days alone in Redding, California, just hanging out at Bethel Church. While there, the church had a conference with Bob Jones, Bobby Conner, and Larry Randolph. During this time, they had a ministry session for staff, which I attended. Bill

Johnson, being the extremely gracious host that he is, encouraged me to go up and get prayer along with his staff. I declined several times because I felt bad interrupting something that was meant for the church staff, but Bill managed to get me up on stage where the ministry was happening. I stayed off to the side, watching people receive ministry, but the hunger that I had to have an encounter with God grew exponentially—to the point where it was tangible in my physical body.

Along with the hunger came a growing sense of the presence of God on me right at that very moment. I have never asked Bill if he remembers this or not, so I don't know what, if anything, he noted, but while my sense of the presence of God intensified, Bill walked up to me and placed his hand on my stomach and it felt like I got punched—HARD. I instantly collapsed onto my knees while tears began gushing from my face. It's very hard to describe what I was sensing at that point. It was some strange combination of feeling like something on the inside of me was exploding, while also feeling like something was resting very heavily on the outside of me. But if I say that it felt like weight, that's not actually a good description. Weight, being an effect of gravity, pushes downward. The weight I was feeling pressed inward. The bottom of me felt like it was being pressed up; the sides, inward; and the top, down. At some point, Bill stopped praying for me and his (now) son-in-law, Gabe Valenzuela, continued, and so did the experience. I don't know how long it lasted, but if I had to take a guess, I'd say it was around 45 minutes.

I have had two very similar experiences since then, but neither were as powerful or lasted as long. After this experience, there was a clear increase in anointing when I ministered to people. Many of those for whom I prayed have had an encounter with the Holy Spirit or have received greater anointing and power when they minister. I have seen an increase in people healed when I pray for them, and my words of knowledge have become more concise.

One of the things that stands out to me, that became much more pronounced, is the number of people who have received impartation in the areas of healing and words of knowledge. As well, I have developed a new passion and clarity when preaching. There is hardly ever a time when I preach that I don't find myself crying, as the Holy Spirit often visits me during this time. When this started, I was a little afraid that the crying would be misunderstood or perceived as something it was not. But to the contrary, people often tell me that in the middle of it, God did something to them that no one would readily associate with seeing someone cry: He healed their bodies, broke demonic mindsets and strongholds, and imparted a passion for the lost, sick, and dying. So, while still somewhat embarrassing, I'll take the public crying in exchange for the fruit and, more importantly, the visitation from the Holy Spirit that accompanies it.[2]

Randy MacMillan

The following is an excerpt from an interview I (Randy Clark) did with the late Randy McMillan in Cali, Colombia, in 2009. I consider this interview one of the most exceptional I have done, and I have done hundreds. I encourage you to view the video of the entire interview, which can be found on YouTube.[3] Randy McMillan was a great prophetic and apostolic leader of the Church. These are his own words:

> I experienced my first healing when I was a teenager. I did not know anything about healing. The whole dimension of the Holy Spirit I had no clue about. After the power of the Holy Spirit came upon me with my vision of the Lord on December 17, 1971, in Jacksonville, Florida, at Jacksonville University, I prayed for healing because I had compassion for people and wanted to see them healed.
>
> On December 17, God called me to a country whose language I did not speak, in the ministry of prophet and

teacher, and He said I would prepare His people for the coming that was very soon. He told me not to hesitate to entertain strangers.

It was the last day of school before the Christmas vacation, and He appeared to me. When I saw Jesus's glory, I was going from the feet up to the face, and when our eyes met, it was like the brightness of the sun. I could not resist, but I just melted. I wept for several hours. I wept for hours for all the sadness and brokenness for everything that I had done.

I saw all the things in people's lives that I hurt, but when you see Jesus, you realize why you are not closer to Him. He is so pure that you have to be willing to melt before Him. There were guys with me in the car, and they heard what I heard. They heard me asking questions to Jesus.

One of my friends said these things can only come from two places, either God or the devil—either that or I was getting a missionary call. The call was very specific.[4]

Years later, I had a prophetic vision, and it woke me up, but I was still seeing what was going on. It was a prophetic vision. It was a vision of the Body of Christ being taken apart, and I was taking the part I wanted, meaning I was not concerned with other people's churches and ministries. That is when I realized that we had to reach the whole city; it could not just be my ministry.

Bob Balassi

The following is an account (not a first-person account) about the experience of Bob Balassi, a former worship leader at St. Louis Vineyard Church. Bob is a successful computer analyst who works in the secular field. He is not prone to emotion and is a logical thinker. Yet Bob's baptism in the Holy Spirit is one of the most inspiring stories I have heard. Here is his story as I recall it: Bob was sick with the stomach flu. Two of his five young children were also sick with the flu. Bob was hugging the commode when he heard his children beginning to throw up also. He said a short prayer about how God could heal his family. Suddenly, his hands began to tingle, then to be electrified. He felt as if his fingers were going to blow off. Then he began to experience a gamut of emotions. He was laughing and then crying as he experienced the glory of God. Kathleen, his wife, came into the bathroom to observe her husband being baptized with the Holy Spirit. Bob had a profound sense of the majesty of God as His glory and splendor filled the bathroom with an overwhelming presence. Praise and petitions filled his mouth. He left the bathroom to go pray for his children. Each was healed, as was Bob.[5]

CONCLUSION

What is the baptism in the Holy Spirit? It is many things. It is the intense presence of Jesus, who will be with you to the end of the age.[1] It is power to witness, which is a Pentecostal emphasis. It is activation of the gifts of the Holy Spirit, which is a Charismatic emphasis. It is power to dominate sin rather than be dominated by sin and a mature love for God and others, which are Holiness emphases. It is a greater love for the Bible, which is an Evangelical emphasis. And it is a greater commitment to the Great Commission, which is valued by Pentecostals, Charismatics, Holiness, Evangelicals, and Catholics alike. If one is Catholic, one also obtains a greater love for the Church and the sacrament of the Eucharist, along with a greater sense of the real presence of Jesus in the life of the one baptized in the Holy Spirit. I am reminded here of what Jon Ruthven said in Chapter 8: "The bottom line, then, is that if we combine these terms, *baptism* and *Holy Spirit*, it seems that the New Testament concept of the baptism in/with/of the Holy Spirit is that one is *immersed or flooded into the power and gifts of God, particularly gifts of revelation, prophecy, utterance, and power.*

My question in closing is this: If Jesus waited until He was anointed with the Holy Spirit before beginning His ministry; if the disciples, after spending three years with Jesus and ministering with Him—in His power and authority—were still told to wait until they were empowered by the Holy Spirit before beginning their ministries; if the history makers in this world for the Kingdom of God, seemed to have had such baptisms in the Spirit; and if in our contemporary context the same seems to be true, who are we to feel that such an experience is not needed? Can we move beyond traditional theology, which, as Jon says, is a *theology of preparation*, a *repent and be baptized*, that denies every goal of this preparation—the charismatic Spirit? "The New Testament, by contrast, sees the ideal as a single package—one's commission, which includes one's 'calling,' the *ordo salutis*, the baptism, and charismatic discipling of others."[2]

Have you had an experience of God's empowering presence? If not, then ask, seek, knock, and you will receive. Let God touch you profoundly in His own way. Don't worry about understanding or being able to correctly theologize what God has done. Instead, become like a little child, having faith that if we who are evil give good gifts to our children, how much more the heavenly Father will give the Holy Spirit to those who ask.[3]

Don't focus on any particular manifestation other than receiving His power and love. Some people have almost no manifestations during the time of their encounter, but afterward notice a difference in their lives and ministry, when more fruit is present and more people are touched through their ministry. Many more who experience God's empowering presence do feel power—so much so that they have physical manifestations such as laughing, crying, shaking-trembling, feeling energy coursing through their bodies, and falling down under God's power. And many have the experience of speaking in tongues.

I believe that when one is baptized and he or she speaks in tongues at the same time, it is a wonderful and valid experience. But this is not always the way it is. Some speak in tongues before they are baptized in the Spirit. Others speak in tongues after they are baptized in the Spirit. And still others receive the baptism in the Spirit and have never spoken in tongues. The experience of tongues isn't emotional and does not always manifest when one is in the midst of what are often powerful emotions present during Holy Spirit baptism; rather, tongues sometimes comes at a time other than when the person was baptized in the Spirit. In these occasions there isn't nearly as much emotions when the experience of tongues occurs as when the person is baptized in the Holy Spirit.

Remember, the Holy Spirit is poured out for many reasons. God pours out His Spirit to empower us for witness, for victory over sin, for activation of the gifts, for greater power in and greater love of the Word, for greater love for the Church, for greater appreciation for the mysteries of His offered grace, and for revelation and illumination, both individually and corporately, into His truths. "The point of the Pentecost story is that the New Covenant is the Spirit of prophecy (speech) equipping disciples for the mission Jesus demonstrated and then gave to them."[4]

Cry out now for God to equip you anew and afresh! His promises lead to the Gospel of Jesus Christ, where you will find His truths revealed and His peace given. It is in Jesus that we are sanctified and justified, washed clean, and, by the power of the precious Holy Spirit, enabled to walk in His power and peace to the glory of His matchless name. *"Call to Me and I will answer you and tell you great and unsearchable things you do not know"* (Jer. 33:3).

Prayers

The major call on my life is to be used by the Holy Spirit to activate the gifts of the Spirit and to pray for people to be baptized or filled with the Holy Spirit. I have two prayers that may help facilitate this process in your life. I suggest that you read each prayer and familiarize yourself with what is being said. Then, if your heart is in agreement, pray. Let the Holy Spirit lead you. He may bring other words to your heart and mind to speak. These prayers are meant to be an aid to you, not a substitute for your words. Don't give up. Believe, and you will receive.

> *Father, I come in the authority of Jesus's name. I thank You for drawing me to Yourself through the conviction of the Holy Spirit.*
>
> *Jesus, I thank You for dying for me at the cross, bearing my sins and the sins of the world. I thank You for also bearing in Your body sickness and disease, so that healing could be released through the laying on of hands and the prayers of Christians. I thank You for bearing the stripes on Your body by which I, and others, could be healed.*
>
> *Jesus, the Bible says that You are the One who baptizes in the Holy Spirit. I ask You to baptize me in the Holy Spirit. I*

ask You to fill me again. I want to walk in the power of the Holy Spirit, bearing the fruit of love, joy, peace, patience, kindness, goodness, faithfulness, gentleness, and self-control. Jesus, I also want to walk in the fruit of being able to ask and to receive in Your name, to walk in faith—faith to step out in the gifts of the Holy Spirit. I want to be able to prophesy, receive and give words of knowledge, and to be used in healing—experiencing the gifts of healings. I want to not only grow in my measure of faith; I want to experience Your gift of faith, a faith that removes doubt, that gives certainty that the mountain I am speaking to is going to move—the kind of faith that results in miracles. I want to be able to set people free who are demonized, aided by the discerning of spirits, and be able, through this same gift, to judge prophecy—whether it is from You, the flesh, or the enemy. I want to be able to speak in tongues, enabling me to build myself up in the Holy Spirit, to make me stronger for Your service. I do not want to be limited in my ability to pray because, when I am not limited, my spirit can be led by Your Spirit as it searches my heart to pray about things my mind does not understand. Lord, I am willing to bring a message in tongues to my church, if You would desire. I ask to be able to interpret messages in tongues so that the people who hear would know and benefit—that they would hear the words of praise and adoration to You offered by the Holy Spirit. I want to experience the gift of the word of wisdom in order to have godly wisdom, to know what to do, to know how to give words of knowledge, to know how and when to bring forth Your prophetic words, to know the timing of when to release them, to have the wisdom to understand the ways of God as well as the timing of God. Jesus, I ask for these gifts from First Corinthians 12. I know that they all are in the Holy Spirit, and He is in me. I ask that these gifts that I have access to through the indwelling

Holy Spirit would be stirred up in me. I know they are not mine; they are Yours—but I also know that I have access to them through my justification. Jesus, I also ask that I would walk in whatever gifts You know I need to fulfill Your purpose for my life. Help me to understand the gifts You have worked in me and to grow in them, seeing my measure of faith grow—whether it is prophesying, serving, teaching, encouraging, giving, leading, or showing mercy. Help me to honor the gifts I see in my Christian brothers and sisters and to encourage them in their gifts.

Holy Spirit, thank You for convicting me of my sins, alerting me to my need of forgiveness and a righteousness that was not my own, not based upon what I had done or how good I was. Thank You for revealing to me the righteousness that comes by faith in Jesus Christ. Thank You that You drew me to the Father through Jesus. Thank You, Holy Spirit, for taking what the Father has made known to Jesus and now revealing this knowledge to me. Thank You for coming inside of me in regeneration in my new birth. I know that You and the Father and Son live in me through Your presence in me.

Holy Spirit, I want more of the triune God in me—more of You, more of Jesus, more of the Father. I want to be conformed to the image of Christ by Your renewing of my mind.

Spirit of the living God, fall afresh on me.

Spirit of the living God, fall afresh on me;

Melt me, mold me, fill me, use me.

Spirit of the living God, fall afresh on me.

Spirit of the living God, fall afresh on me.

Spirit of the living God, fall afresh on me;

Melt me, mold me, fill me, use me.

Spirit of the living God, fall afresh on me;

Fall afresh on me.

Holy Spirit, I need Your sanctifying work in my heart. Come and set me free from sins that I have not been able to overcome, that bring me shame and guilt. I'm thankful that I can approach the throne of grace to receive mercy and forgiveness, but I ask for Your power to become victorious over those sins in my life that are causing me to stumble, that compromise my witness to Christ. I believe there is such an experience of power in You that I can become victorious in my walk with Christ. I want to walk in the fullness of the Spirit. I want to experience all that Jesus suffered and died for. I want to receive all the rewards of the Lamb that was slain.

Almighty God—Father, Son, and Holy Spirit—grant me a broken and contrite heart over my weakness and sin, create a new heart within me, and give me a willing spirit. Lift me up out of the muddy pit, set my feet upon the Rock, and put a new song in my heart.

Lord God, I am willing to do whatever You want me to do. Make me a coin in Your pocket and spend me any way You want. God, I want to become Your ambassador of reconciliation and Your witness by my words and by my life.

God, baptize me in Your Spirit. Let me burn with the fire of Your presence.

I surrender my life totally to You and believe as I lay my life on Your altar, Your fire will come down and consume this offering.

If there is something in this prayer that you cannot honestly pray but you would like to be able to pray, I suggest that you begin with the following prayer:

Lord, I want to be willing to pray this commitment, but I know there is a struggle in my heart, so I ask You to change my heart and make me willing. I want to be willing. I want to be filled; I want a first-time or a fresh baptism in the Holy Spirit.

This prayer may be something you could pray right now, or there may be parts of it that you can't pray today. But as you keep crying out to God, He can bring you to the place of being able to pray the prayer in full.

Now, I want to pray for you, for you to receive. This is not a time for you to pray in your own words but a time for you to speak these words of prayer over your life. If there is something you are not open to because of a theological position, simply do not speak that part of my blessing over yourself.

Father, in the name of Jesus, I bless (say your name). I pray for the Holy Spirit to come upon (say your name). Fill him/her with Your power. I pray for gifts of the Spirit within to be stirred up. I pray for the activation of the gifts of the Spirit to happen in (say your name). I call forth those gifts that will be needed to accomplish Your will and Your call on (say your name) life. Come, Holy Spirit, release Your energy. May the power of Your presence descend upon (say your name). Electricity, energy, heat, power, love, holy tears, joyous laughter—Father, whatever way You choose to manifest Your empowering presence, let it come now. I pray for a baptism of love and a baptism of power.

Jesus, mighty Baptizer in the Holy Spirit, I bless (say your name). I pray for Your power to overwhelm (say your name). I pray for Your love to come so powerfully that holy tears are given to (say your name). I pray for Your peace to overwhelm (say your name). May he or she rest in your peace. I pray for the joy of Your Spirit to come upon (say your name). May it be so strong that holy laughter is experienced. I pray for (say your name) that he/she may experience tongues, or tongues and prophecy.[1]

In the mighty name of Jesus and in the authority of His name, I bless (say your name). Amen.

APPENDIX

Summary

1. There is biblical evidence of God baptizing, filling, sanctifying, and empowering people in various ways, with various phenomena or manifestations, and producing various levels of fruit in their lives. See 12-13, 52-58, 100, 132.

2. There is historical evidence of such diversity in the history of the Church. See pages 66-67, 92, 96-97, 101-102, 109, 174-184.

3. There is contemporary evidence of diversity of timing—whether baptism in the Spirit is simultaneous with conversion or subsequent to conversion; difference in regard to the relationship to water baptism; and difference in regard to the issue of evidence; power, tongues, tears, joy, peace, laughter, prophecy, bold proclamation, or combinations thereof. See pages 22-25, 30-33, 46.

4. The history of revival is connected to the history of people who were desiring to experience more of God. See pages 93, 173-174, 187-199.

5. The baptism in the Spirit or filling of the Spirit should not be seen as an optional add-on to salvation; it is necessary for victorious living. See pages 25, 131, 143.

6. The early Church saw the laying on of hands for the filling or

baptism in the Spirit to be an important part of the conversion-initiation process, and saw this prayer with the laying on of hands as part of the baptismal event. It was to follow baptism. Baptism made the person holy and fit to receive the filling of the Spirit. See pages 57, 70, 71, 75-76, 80, 83-85.

7. This pattern has continued up until this day. See 89, 91, 95, 100.

8. The Pentecostal experience as subsequent to justification is supported by the liturgy of the ancient Church and in contemporary liturgy. See 83-84, 89.

9. Pentecostals' exegesis of the Bible for the support of their doctrine is not as solid as they have believed in the past. See 46, 52, 55, 60-62, 64-65, 135.

10. The Pentecostal experience is much more solidly portrayed in Scripture than has been believed in the past by Evangelicals. See page 56, 62-65, 132-138, 157-158.

11. The baptism in the Holy Spirit is at the heart of the New Covenant. And the New Covenant is the primary emphasis of the Bible. See 133-135, 139-141, 145-146, 153, 156, 158-159, 207.

12. The Trinity is very much part of being baptized in the Holy Spirit. See page 122, 125, 153.

13. John Wesley seems to be the Protestant who has the most accurate biblical understanding of the various dispensations of the Holy Spirit in the life of a believer. See 23, 57-58, 91-96.

14. Wesley is the connection between Catholicism and Pentecostalism and is the "grandfather" of the Pentecostal and Charismatic movements. See 78, 94-96.

15. God is sovereign and can break out of the normal *ordo salutis* and do whatever He wants in whatever means He chooses. See pages 58, 135-136, 206.

16. Everyone should desire to be filled or baptized with/in the Holy Spirit. See pages 26, 35, 65, 116-117, 206-207.

Notes

Introduction

1. Mary Healy, e-mail message to author, October 31, 2016 and subsequent e-mail message to author, November 15, 2016.

2. Frederick Dale Bruner, *A Theology of the Holy Spirit* (Grand Rapids, MI: William B. Eerdmans, 1970), 92, 323–41.

3. Tom Jones, "Divine Encounters: Analysis of Encounters that Shape Lives" (D.Min. dissertation, United Theological Seminary, 2013), 129.

4. Randy Clark, *Changed in a Moment* (Mechanicsburg, PA: Global Awakening, 2010), 132.

5. Lawrence W. Wood, *The Meaning of Pentecost in Early Methodism* (Lanham, MD: Scarecrow Press, 2002), 8-10.

6. Paulos Hanfere, e-mail message to author, July 15, 2015.

7. Rich Nathan and Ken Wilson, *Empowered Evangelicals: Bringing Together the Best of the Evangelical and Charismatic Worlds* (Ann Arbor, MI: Servant Publications, 1995), 11.

8. F. F. Bosworth, *Christ the Healer* (Grand Rapids, MI: Chosen Books, 2000), 101.

Chapter 1
The Evangelical, Holiness, Pentecostal, and Catholic Perspectives on the Baptism in the Holy Spirit

1. Paul Pavao, "Holy Spirit Baptism Quotes." *Christian History for Everyman*, last modified 2014, accessed August 18, 2016, http://www.christian-history.org/holy-spirit-baptism-quotes .html.

2. Lewis Drummond, ed., *What the Bible Says: A Systematic Guide to Biblical Doctrines* (Nashville, TN: Abingdon Press, 1975), 78. Emphasis added.

3. R. A. Torrey, *The Holy Spirit: Who He Is and What He Does* (Alachua, FL: Bridge-Logos, 2008), 121.

4. Ibid., 124–27.

5. A. T. Pierson, *The Keswick Movement: In Precept and Practice* (New York: Funk and Wagnall's, 1903).

6. For more information see Brittany Smith, "More Than 1 in 4 Christians Are Pentecostal, Charismatic," *Christian Post Reporter*, December 21, 2011, accessed October 31, 2016, http://www.christianpost.com/news/ more-than-1-in-4-christians-are-pentecostal-charismatic-65358/.

7. Assemblies of God, *Our 16 Fundamental Truths*, March 1, 2010, accessed December 28, 2016, http://www.ag.org/ top/beliefs/statement_of_fundamental_truths/sft_full.cfm, emphasis added.

8. George O. Wood, "From the General Superintendent," *Assemblies of God*, accessed August 18, 2016, http:// agchurches.org/Sitefiles/Default/RSS/AG.org%20TOP/ WoodRevivalStatement.pdf.

9. David B. Barrett, ed., "Pentecostalism," *World Christian Encyclopedia: A Comparative Survey of Churches and Religions in the Modern World, A.D. 1900–2000*, 1st ed., (Oxford, UK: Oxford University Press, 1982).

10. A. J. Gordon, *The Ministry of the Spirit* (Philadelphia, PA: Judson Press, 1984), 72. Gordon was a Baptist pastor and one of the leaders of the 19ᵗʰ-century Faith Cure movement. He was also part of the Holiness movement—from the Keswick emphasis more than the Wesleyan Holiness emphasis.

11. Glenn Clark, "Jennie Evans Moore Seymour—Vanguard of Pentecost," *Charisma Magazine*, November 30, 2003, http://www.charismamag.com/site-archives/24-uncategorised/9826-jennie-evans-moore-seymour-vanguard-of-pentecost.

12. International Catholic Charismatic Renewal Services (ICCRS), *Baptism in the Holy Spirit* (Vatican City, Italy: Doctrinal Commission of ICCRS, 2012), 13.

13. Ibid., 14.

14. Kilian McDonnell and George T. Montague, eds., *Fanning the Flame: What Does Baptism in the Holy Spirit Have to Do with Christian Initiation?* (Collegeville, MN: Liturgical Press, 1991), 10.

15. Ibid., 21.

16. Ibid., 15.

17. Ibid., 22.

18. Ibid., 27.

19. Heidi Baker, "Pentecostal Experience: Towards a Reconstructive Theology of Glossolalia" (Ph.D. dissertation, King's College, 158).

20. Yves Congar, *I Believe in the Holy Spirit,* translated by David Smith (New York: Crossroad, 2005), 94.

21. William J. O'Shea, *Sacraments of Initiation* (Englewood Cliffs, NJ: Prentice-Hall, 1965), 65. I like to use the following language in my teaching: "God wants to give us the experiential truth of walking in righteousness through sanctification or baptism in the Spirit of our imputed righteousness that came in justification. He desires to make holy what He calls holy by the power of His Spirit."

22. Congar, *I Believe*, 189.

23. Raniero Cantalamessa, *Sober Intoxication of the Spirit: Filled with the Fullness of God* (Cincinnati, OH: Servant Books, 2005), 159.

24. Francis MacNutt, "My Search for the Spirit," *Christian Healing Ministries*, Spring 2014, accessed August 18, 2016, https://www.christianhealingmin.org/index.php?option=com _content&view=article&id=626:my-search-for-the-spirit& catid=209&Itemid=458.

25. Thomas Kidd, "'More a Doctrine Than a Person': Evangelicals and the Holy Spirit," *The Anxious Bench*, December 2, 2014, accessed August 8, 2016, http:// www.patheos.com/blogs/anxiousbench/2014/12/ more-a-doctrine-than-a-person-evangelicals-and-the-holy-spirit/.

Chapter 2
The Traditional and Recent Pentecostal Perspectives of the Baptism in the Holy Spirit

1. William W. Menzies, *Anointed to Serve: The Story of the Assemblies of God* (Springfield, MO: Gospel Publishing House, 1980), 388.

2. Léon-Joseph Suenens, *A New Pentecost?*, translated by Francis Martin (New York: Seabury Press, 1975), 80–81.

3. ICCRS, *Baptism*, 30.

4. Ibid., 32.

5. Ibid., 33.

6. John Piper, "You Will Be Baptized with the Holy Spirit," Sermon, September 23, 1990, accessed August 18, 2016, www.desiringgod.org/sermons/ you-will-be-baptized-with-the-holy-spirit.

7. Tommy Welchel and Michelle P. Griffith, *True Stories of the Miracles of Azusa Street and Beyond* (Shippensburg, PA: Destiny Image, 2013), 55, 107.

8. The year was 1998, and Tony Campolo and I were the two main speakers. See Tony Campolo, *Stories That Feed Your Soul* (Grand Rapids, MI: Baker, 2014), 90.

9. Piper, "You Will Be Baptized."

10. Ibid.

11. Frank D. Macchia, *Baptized in the Spirit: A Global Pentecostal Theology* (Grand Rapids, MI: Zondervan, 2006), 60.

12. Henry I. Lederle, *Theology with Spirit: The Future of the Pentecostal & Charismatic Movements in the 21ˢᵗ Century* (Tulsa, OK: Word & Spirit Press, 2010), 172, e-book, 281n45.

13. Ibid.

14. Macchia, *Baptized*, 77.

15. Lederle, *Theology*, 172.

16. Ibid., 172–73.

17. Ibid., 173–74.

18. Don Basham, *A Handbook on Holy Spirit Baptism* (Monroeville, PA: Whitaker Books, 1969), 11.

19. Ibid., 11–13.

20. Tommy Tyson, "Biography," *Tommy Tyson*, accessed August 18, 2016, http://www.tommytyson.org/index.php?option=com _content&view=article&id=51&Itemid=55.

21. Francis MacNutt, "Being Baptized in the Holy Spirit," *Tentmaker*, May/June 2003, accessed August 7, 2016, http:// www.tentmaker.org/holy-spirit/baptized.htm.

Chapter 3
The Scriptural Basis for the Traditional Pentecostal and Evangelical Positions Considered

1. ICCRS, *Baptism*, 41.

2. Asa Mahan, *Baptism of the Holy Spirit* (Clifton, NY: Williams Publishers, 1880), 63–64.

3. James Dunn, *Baptism in the Holy Spirit: A Re-examination of the New Testament Teaching on the Gift of the Spirit in Relation to Pentecostalism Today* (Philadelphia, PA: The Westminster Press, 1970), 66–67.

4. See Michael Green, *Evangelism in the Early Church* (Grand Rapids, MI: Eerdmans, 2003).

5. Mahan, *Baptism*, 66–67.

6. Dunn, *Baptism*, 86.

7. Dunn, *Baptism*, 87.

8. Basham, *Handbook*, 96.

9. R. A. Torrey, *The Baptism with the Holy Spirit* (Minneapolis, MN: Bethany Fellowship, 1972), 30.

10. Kilian McDonnell and Arnold Bittlinger, *The Baptism in the Holy Spirit as an Ecumenical Problem* (Notre Dame, IN: Charismatic Renewal Services, 1972), 11–12, 19–20. See also Robert H. Culpepper, *Evaluating the Charismatic Movement—A Theological and Biblical Appraisal* (Valley Forge, PA: Judson Press, 1977), 59

11. Culpepper, *Evaluating*, 59.

12. Gordon D. Fee, *Gospel and Spirit: Issues in New Testament Hermeneutics* (Peabody, MA: Hendrickson Publishers, 1991), 106–107. The following quotes are used here with permission.

13. Ibid., 108.

14. Ibid., 110–11. Emphasis added.

15. Ibid., 116.

16. Ibid., 117–18.

17. Ibid., 118.

18. Ibid., 118.

19. Ibid., 119.

20. Ibid., 119. Emphasis added.

21. J. D. Greear, "The Most Important Thing About the Holy Spirit," interview by Jen Pollock Michel, *Christianity Today*, January 5, 2015.

22. Bob DeWaay, "Mike Bickle and International House of Prayer: The Latter Rain Redivivus," *Critical Issues Commentary 107*, July/August 2008, accessed December 28, 2016, http://cicministry.org/commentary/issue107.htm.

Chapter 4
Baptism in the Holy Spirit

1. Theophilus, *To Autolycus*, 1.12, translated by Marcus Dods. Reproduced on *New Advent*, accessed November 8, 2016, http://www.newadvent.org/fathers/02041.htm.

2. Tertullian, "Homily on Baptism," edited and translated by Ernest Evans, *Tertullian.org*, 1964, accessed October 31, 2016, www.tertullian.org/articles/evans_bapt/evans_bapt_index.htm. I want to emphasize that the anointing is after baptism.

3. Dunn, *Baptism*, vii.

4. Tertullian, *Tertullian's Treatises: Concerning Prayer, Concerning Baptism,* translated by Alexander Soutner (New York: Macmillan Company, 1919), 54.

5. George Montague and Kilian McDonnell, *Christian Initiation and Baptism in the Holy Spirit: Evidence from the First Eight Centuries* (Collegeville, MN: Liturgical, 1994), 108.

6. Don Hanson, *Knowing the Holy Ghost*, 2nd ed. (n.p., 2007), 70.

7. Origen, "Homilies 1–14 on Ezekiel" in *Ancient Christian Writers* (Washington, DC: Catholic University Press, 2001), 103.

8. James Gilchrist Lawson, *Deeper Experiences of Famous Christians* (Anderson, IN: The Warner Press, 1911), 54.

9. Cyprian, *Epistle 72.9 to Stephanus* (Oxford, 73.9), *ANF* 5:381, as cited in Lawson, *Deeper Experiences*.

10. Cyprian, *Epistle 72.12 to Jubaianus, Concerning the Baptism of Heretics*, translated by Robert Ernest Wallis. Reproduced in *New Advent*, accessed November 8, 2016, http://www.newadvent.org/fathers/050672.htm.

11. Cyprian, *Epistle 74 to Cornelius*, translated by Robert Ernest Wallis. Reproduced in *New Advent*, accessed November 8, 2016, http://www.newadvent.org/fathers/050674.htm.

12. Eusebius, *Church History 6.43*, translated by Arthur Cushman McGiffert. Reproduced in *New Advent*, accessed November 8, 2016, http://www.newadvent.org/fathers/250106.htm.

13. The Latin phrase "Qui autem confirmat not vobiscum in Christum et qui unxit nos Deus" translates into English as "Now he that confirmeth us with you in Christ and that hath anointed us, is God," and "et qui signavit nos et dedit pignus Spiritus in ordibus nostris" translates as "Who also hath sealed us and given the pledge of the Spirit in our hearts."

14. Melchiades quoted in Thomas Aquinas, *The Summa Theologiae of St. Thomas Aquinas*, 2nd ed., 3.72, translated by the Fathers of the English Dominican Province. Reproduced in *New Advent*, accessed November 8, 2016, http://www.newadvent .org/summa/4072.htm.

15. Gratian, "On the Holy Spirit," in *On Consecration* 5, as quoted in Lawson, *Deeper Experiences*.

16. Eusebius Emesenus, "Sermon on Pentecost" in *Corpus Christianorum, Series Latina* (CCSL 101:338).

17. Gregory Nazianzen, as quoted in Right Rev. Reginald Herber, *The Whole Works of the Right Rev. Jeremy Taylor, D.D., Lord Bishop of Down, Connor, and Dromore: With a Life of the Author, and a Critical Examination of His Writings,* Vol. 5 (Oxford, England, 1828), 283.

18. See Ambrose, *On the Mysteries*, translated by H. de Romestin, E. de Romestin, and H. T. F. Duckworth. Reproduced in *New Advent*, accessed November 8, 2016, http://www.newadvent .org/fathers/3405.htm.

19. St. John Chrysostom, Commentary on Hebrews 6:1–2.

20. See response 9 in Jerome's *The Dialogue Against the Luciferians*, translated by W. H. Fremantle, G. Lewis, and W. G. Martley. Reproduced in *New Advent*, accessed November 8, 2016, http://www.newadvent.org/fathers/3005.htm.

21. Cyril, *Lectures* 3.21, translated by Edwin Hamilton Gifford. Reproduced in *New Advent*, accessed November 8, 2016, http://www.newadvent.org/fathers/310103.htm.

22. Augustine, *Sermon XXI: The Blasphemy Against the Holy Ghost*, translated by R. G. MacMullen. Reproduced in *New Advent*, accessed November 8, 2016, http://www.newadvent.org/fathers/160321.htm.

23. Alastair H. B. Logan, "Marcellus of Ancyra and Anti-Arian Polemic," *Studia Patristica*, edited by Elizabeth A. Livingstone (Leuven, Belgium: Peeters Press, 1989), 22.189. This quote is paraphrased.

24. Leo the Great, Letter to Nicetas, *Epistle LXXXIX* 7.

25. John Paul II, *On the Holy Spirit in the Life of the Church and the World*, accessed December 28, 2016, http://w2.vatican.va/content/john-paul-ii/en/encyclicals/documents/hf_jp-ii_enc_18051986_dominum-et-vivificantem.html.

26. Congar, *I Believe In the Holy Spirit*, 94.

27. Ibid.

28. Ibid.

29. See Jeremy Taylor, *A Discourse of Confirmation* (Ann Arbor, MI: Text Creation Partnership, 2012).

Chapter 5
Baptism in the Holy Spirit: Protestant and Catholic Perspective

1. Herber, *The Whole Works of the Right Rev. Jeremy Taylor*, 667.

2. "Documents of the Second Ecumenical Council A.D. 381," 7, translated by Henry R. Percival. Reproduced on Orthodoxia. org, accessed November 8, 2016, http://www.orthodoxa.org/GB/orthodoxy/canonlaw/canons2econcileGB.htm.

3. *The Work Claiming to Be the Constitutions of the Holy Apostles*, translated by Irah Chase (New York: D. Appleton, 1848), 143.

4. Ibid., 158.

5. Ibid., 184.

6. Popes and the Charismatic Renewal, accessed December 28, 2016, http://www.lovecrucified.com/holy_spirit/charismatic_renewal/renewal_message_popes.html.

7. Holy Father's Speech for the World Congress of Ecclesial Movements and New Communities, accessed December 28, 2016, http://www.vatican.va/roman _curia/pontifical_councils/laity/documents/rc_pc _laity_doc_27051998_movements-speech-hf_en.html.

8. Pope Saint John Paul II, Vigil of Pentecost, May 29, 2004.

9. Mark Mallett, "More on the Gifts of Tongues," The Now World, accessed December 28, 2016, http://www .markmallett .com/blog/more-on-the-gift-of-tongues/.

10. Pope Invites a Rediscovery of Baptism's Beauty, Zenit: The World Seen from Rome, May 11, 2008, accessed December 28, 2016, https://zenit.org/articles/ pope-invites-a-rediscovery-of-baptism-s-beauty/.

11. "Charismatic Movement—Vatican Promotion." YouTube, accessed October 28, 2016, https://www.youtube.com/ watch?v=J-QDOcDGDWA. All quotes in this subsection preceding this quote are based upon this YouTube promotion of the Roman Catholic Church.

12. Pope Francis quoted in Deacon Keith A. Fournier, "A Current of Grace: Address of Pope Francis to the Charismatic Renewal Conference in Rome." Catholic Online, accessed October 28, 2016, http://www.catholic.org/news/international/europe/story. php?id=55674.

13. Ronald Lawler, Donald Wuerl, and Thomas Comerford Lawler, eds., *The Teaching of Christ: A Catholic Catechism for Adults,* 2nd ed. (Huntington, IN: Our Sunday Visitor, Inc., 2004), 463–64.

14. See Suenens, A New Pentecost?; Father Raniero Cantalamessa, "Concerning the Baptism in the Holy Spirit," Catholic Charismatic Renewal of New Orleans, accessed November 8, 2016, https://www.ccrno.org/WhatisBaptism.php; and Harold Cohen, "Baptized in the Holy Spirit," Catholic Charismatic Renewal of New Orleans, accessed November 8, 2016, https:// www.ccrno.org/WhatisBaptism.php.

15. Cohen, "Baptized." The website on which Cohen's article appears recommends those interested in a fuller theological reflection on the subject read Father Killian McDonnell and George Montague's Christian Initiation and Baptism in the Holy Spirit: Evidence from the First Eight Centuries.

Chapter 6
Baptism in the Holy Spirit: The Holiness and Pentecostal Perspectives

1. Clare George Weakley Jr., *The Nature of Revival: John Wesley, Charles Wesley and George Whitefield* (Minneapolis, MN: Bethany House Publishers, 1987), 79.

2. John Telford, *The Life of John Wesley* (London, UK: The Epworth Press, 1930), 394.

3. Richard Green, *John Wesley—Evangelist.* Reproduced on *Wesley Center Online,* accessed November 1, 2016, http://wesley.nnu.edu/john-wesley/john-wesley-evangelist/john-wesley-evangelist-chapter-6/.

4. Wood, *The Meaning of Pentecost,* 189–98. See also Stanley Burgess, ed., *Christian Peoples of the Spirit: A Documentary History of Pentecostal Spirituality from the Early Church to the Present* (New York: New York University Press, 2011).

5. Baker, Pentecostal Experience, 108.

6. Ibid., 109.

7. Wood, *Meaning,* 188.

8. Ibid., 122.

9. Ibid., 123.

10. Ibid., 163.

11. Ibid., 163.

12. Ibid., 19.

13. Ibid., 125–26.

14. Ibid., 117.

15. Ibid., 131.

16. Vinson Synan, *The Holiness-Pentecostal Movement in the United States* (Grand Rapids, MI: William B. Eerdmans, 1971), 25.

17. H. Orton Wiley, *Christian Theology.* Reproduced in *Wesley Center Online,* accessed November 11, 2016, http://wesley.nnu.edu/noncanonical-literature/henry-orton-wiley/h-orton-wiley-christian-theology-chapter-29/.

18. Charles Finney, *Charles G. Finney: An Autobiography* (Old Tappan, NJ: Fleming H. Revell Company, 1876), 20–21.

19. Ibid., 20.

20. See Thomas Kidd, *George Whitefield: America's Spiritual Founding Father* (Princeton, NJ: Yale University Press, 2014).

21. Leo G. Cox, *John Wesley's Concept of Sin,* accessed December 28, 2016, https://biblicalstudies.org.uk/pdf/bets/vol05/5-1_cox.pdf.

22. Steven Barabas, *So Great Salvation: The History and Message of the Kewsick Convention* (Eugene, OR: Wipf & Stock, 1952), 22.

23. Basham, *Handbook,* 53.

24. See Leona Frances Choy's *Powerlines: What Great Evangelicals Believed About the Holy Spirit, 1850–1930* (Christian Publications, 1990), which records the expressions of the Spirit in many famous Evangelicals.

25. Basham, *Handbook,* 56.

Chapter 7
Receiving the Baptism in the Holy Spirit

1. Ron Phillips, *An Essential Guide to Baptism in the Holy Spirit* (Lake Mary, FL: Charisma House, 2011), 53.

2. Ibid., 55–59.

3. Ibid., 63–68.

4. Ibid, 5.

5. Ibid., 1–8.

6. Paul Martini, e-mail message to author, July 20, 2015.

7. Here Martin is quoting Fee's *Gospel and Spirit,* pg. 864.

8. Dr. Martin sent me this testimony in an email not long after having this experience.

9. Graham, *Holy Spirit*, 107.

10. Torrey, *The Baptism with the Holy Spirit*, 39.

11. Ibid., 44.

12. Ibid., 52.

13. A. W. Tozer, *How to Be Filled with the Holy Spirit* (Camp Hill, PA: Christian Publications, n.d.), 39.

14. Speaking this language is not explicitly discussed by Torrey or Tozer, and I do not believe that one must necessarily speak in tongues to have been filled, although I do believe it is a common sign of baptism.

15. Basham, *Handbook*, 100–09. I believe we should seek multiple baptisms, events that can occur, in my opinion, many times over.

16. Gordon, *Ministry*, 74.

17. Ibid.

18. Harold B. Smith, ed., *Pentecostals from the Inside Out* (London, UK: Victor Books, 1990), 12.

19. Baker, Pentecostal Experience, 171–72.

20. ICCRS, *Baptism*, 78.

21. Ibid., 79.

22. Ibid., 81.

23. Ibid., 82.

24. Ibid., 84.

25. Baker, Pentecostal Experience, 156.

26. Joseph Bentivegna and S.J. Messina, "The Witness of St. Augustine on the Action of the Holy Spirit in the Church and the Praxis of Charismata in His Times," *Studia Patristica*, Vol. 22, Edited by Elizabeth A. Livingstone (Leuven, Belgium: Peeters Press, 1989), 189.

27. See Mary Crawford, *The Shantung Revival* (Mechanicsburg, PA, Apostolic Network of Global Awakening, 2005).

Chapter 8
It Is the Spirit Who Testifies

1. Will Hart, e-mail message to author, January 11, 2016.

Chapter 9
The Central Mission and Message of Jesus

1. John Wimber, *Power Healing* (San Francisco, CA: HarperCollins, 1987), 9.

2. Luther stated: "Faith should not rest on signs and wonders alone but on the Word. For signs and wonders may actually be false and untrue; but he who builds on the Word cannot be deceived, because God's promise is certain and cannot lie. Although the Lord performed signs and wonders in order to let Himself be seen and move people to faith, He nonetheless wanted people to look more at the Word than at the signs, which were intended to serve as a testimony to the Word. For it was not His main purpose to give this or that sick person bodily aid; it was His most important office to direct people to the Word and to impress it on their hearts, so that they should be saved thereby." E. Plass, *Luther's Works* (St. Louis, MO: Concordia, 1957–88), 13a, 942f.

   Luther further taught that "the miracles of Christianity are like bells which announce that the preaching church service is about to begin. But when it has begun, they cease to ring, having served their purpose. So the miracles of the New Testament era called attention to the fact that the completed redemption was about to be proclaimed" (957). Clearly the Reformers saw the Gospel as a purely verbal phenomenon, resulting in a "faith" commitment to a creed—"Jesus died for your sins"—resulting in "salvation." Miracles could only serve as "proofs," to "confirm" the preached Word, instead of being, as the New Testament shows, *the characteristic way God reveals Himself* (Heb. 2:4) *as the Gospel* (Rom. 15:18-19; 2 Cor. 12:12).

Calvin, for his part, writes: "In demanding miracles of us they act dishonestly. For we are not forging some new gospel, but are retaining that very gospel whose truth all the miracles that Jesus Christ and His disciples ever wrought *serve to confirm*." See the John Calvin, "Prefatory Address" in *Institutes of the Christian Religion*, 16.

3. See Luke 4:18; Rom. 15:18-19.

4. Jon Ruthven, *What's Wrong with Protestant Theology? Tradition vs. Biblical Emphasis* (Tulsa, OK: Word & Spirit Press, 2013), 336.

5. See Matt. 3:11; Mark 1:8; Luke 3:16; 4:18; John 1:26,33; Rom. 15:8.

6. See Isa. 61:1-2; Acts 10:38; 1 Cor. 11:1; 2 Cor. 4:8-16; Phil. 3:17; 1 Tim. 3:16; 1 Pet. 2:21-24; 3:18.

7. See Mark 3:14-15; Matt. 10; Mark 6; Luke 9; 10; and continuing the imitation process: 1 Cor. 4:16; 1:11; 1 Thess. 1:5-6; 2 Tim. 3:10; Heb. 6:12.

8. See Matt. 26:28-29; Mark 14:24-25; Luke 22:20, 1 Cor. 11:25; Gal. 3:10-16; Heb. 9:15; 10:10; 12:24; 13:20-21.

9. See Rom. 1:4-5; Phil. 3:10-14; Rom. 8:11-14; 1 Tim. 3:16.

10. See John 14:16-18,26; 16:7; Acts 2:33,39; Isa. 59:21; Eph. 4:7-11.

11. See John 14:18; 14:26; 1 Cor. 15:45; 2 Cor. 3:17.

12. See also Mark 1:8; Luke 3:16; Acts 11:16.

13. See also Heb. 9:15.

14. Geza Vermes, *Jesus the Jew: A Historian's Reading of the Gospels* (Philadelphia, PA: Fortress Press, 1973), 78–82.

Chapter 10
Where Is the Cross of Jesus in All of This?

1. See Jer. 31:33.

2. See Isa. 59:21; Acts 2:39.

3. See also Deut. 28.

4. I (Randy Clark) do not disagree that Jon's interpretation of the passage is a possible meaning regarding the division in the Church over the healing dimension, but I think we should not limit this passage's possible interpretations to Jon's alone. There is, in my opinion, reason to interpret the passage in another way, one that is more sacramental than Jon's position. By not discerning the material body, we could fail to discern the significance of Jesus's body in which He bore our sicknesses and diseases and by whose stripes we are healed (see Isa. 53:5). Understanding the power of the blood creates faith for salvation. Understanding the body creates faith for healing. Therefore, not discerning the physical body in this passage could mean a failure to understand the fullness of the Good News. God has provided not only salvation from sins, but also healing for our diseases and infirmities.

5. See the forthcoming work by Jon Ruthven, *How Protestants Rewrote the Bible*, an examination of key terms in the New Testament that were radically redefined by the Protestant Reformation. See also an outstanding article by James Dunn, "Spirit and Kingdom," in *Expository Times* 80, no. 2 (1970): 36–40, which both distinguishes between these New Testament terms and also shows their intimate, almost synonymous, connection.

6. Emphasis added by Randy Clark.

7. Dunn points out a "classic example" of such a detachment of the dogmatic description of the Spirit from that of Scripture is the article on the Holy Spirit in the *Encyclopedia Britannica* (1964, vol. 2) "which confines its treatment to three subjects—Divinity, Procession and Personality of the Holy Spirit—and seems to assume that no more need be said" (7). See Dunn, "Rediscovering the Spirit" in *Expository Times* 84, no. 1 (October 1972).

8. Jon Ruthven, *On the Cessation of the Charismata: The Protestant Polemic on Postbiblical Miracles* (Tulsa, OK: Word & Spirit Press, 2011) and "Appendix on the Essentially Charismatic Nature of the Spirit's Activity" (Ph.D. dissertation, Marquette University, 1989), 315–23. Dunn writes in his entry on "Spirit in the New Testament" in the *New International Dictionary of New Testament Theology* (Grand Rapids, MI: Zondervan, 1999): "For the first Christians, the Spirit was most characteristically a divine power manifesting itself in inspired utterance" (699).

9. We must distinguish here between "biblical" and "systematic" theologians. The movement of "Biblical theology" started in Europe in the 1930s in response to Karl Barth's monumental reaction to old liberalism that had denied the Bible as *the* source of Christian faith. Barth wanted a return to the Protestant orthodoxy of *sola scriptura, sola Christi,* etc. Scholars then began to focus on Scripture, *"allowing it to speak with its own voice"* instead of imposing highly derivative, evolved human dogma on its pages, as was the practice historically. One great product of this movement was the definitive, ten-volume *Theological Dictionary of the New Testament* edited by Gerhard Kittel. An Old Testament version is in production. Another good source is Colin Brown (ed.), *New International Dictionary of New Testament Theology* (Grand Rapids, MI: Zondervan, 1986) and Willem VanGemeren's even larger Old Testament version. Despite their goal of seeking the meaning of *biblical* terms, a traditional bias often seeps into these latter works— especially about Charismatic issues.

    Systematic theology is a continually evolving and highly organized treatment of what is believed to be the essence of the Christian message filling out the structural skeleton of the Creeds. Examples are Thomas Aquinas's *Summa Theologica* (1274), Calvin's *Institutes of the Christian Religion* (1536), and Barth's major work, *Church Dogmatics* (1957). Of course there are hundreds of "systematic theologies" out there but none that I know of that are based on the mission and message of Jesus to His disciples as explicitly stated in the New Testament: *"He will baptize you with the Holy Spirit"* (Matt. 3:11; Mark 1:8; Luke 3:16). Overwhelmingly, traditional systematic theology bypasses the New Testament emphasis on Jesus inaugurating the Kingdom of God in power and commissioning that to His disciples. Systematic theologians remain incurious about the good results of biblical theology.

10. Peter Moore, "God Told Me To, Say 38% of Americans," *YouGov*, October 25, 2013, accessed August 18, 2016, https://today.yougov.com/news/2013/10/25/god-told-me/.

11. The Harris Poll #11, February 26, 2003.

12. The Harris Poll #90, December 14, 2005.

13. The survey was conducted by HCD Research and the Louis Finkelstein Institute for Religious and Social Studies of the Jewish Theological Seminary in New York on December 23, 2004. Interestingly, an Israeli survey, published at the end of 2008, claimed that 82 percent of Jews believed in miracles and that 41 percent claimed to experience miracles of their own. The Ynet-Gesher poll was conducted by the Panels Research Institute and included 500 respondents constituting a representative sample of the adult Jewish population in Israel. For the widespread awareness of miracles around the world, see Craig S. Keener's excellent study, *Miracles: The Credibility of the New Testament Accounts* (Grand Rapids, MI: Baker Academic, 2011).

14. See Rom. 9:1; 2 Cor. 1:12; 5:11; 1 Tim. 1:19; Heb. 10:22.

15. See Matt. 28:20; cf. John 14:18,28; 2 Cor. 3:17.

16. Not the awkward, incorrect, and irrelevant translation that appears in most Bibles: "When the Day of Pentecost had fully come." Luke's title shows that his intention was to show *how* the Day of Pentecost (commemoration of the covenant—originally the offer of God's voice) was fulfilled.

17. See Heb. 12:18-25.

18. By contrast to the clear scriptural teaching itself, the Reformation tradition (Luther, Calvin) saw the written Word as *superior* to revelation. Luther said of his charismatic opponent, Thomas Müntzer, that he wouldn't believe Müntzer prophecies "even if he had swallowed the Holy Spirit feathers and all!" Was Luther saying here that he rejected the gift of prophecy even if he knew it was the Spirit speaking?

Luther here is apparently overreacting to Müntzer's radical position on the Holy Spirit. Müntzer believed, as many in the Radical Reformation did, that along with Papal Encyclicals, Creeds, and all "man-made" religious documents, the Bible should be thrown out as well, depending only on the "inner light" or witness of the Spirit. In reacting to Müntzer, Luther threw out the baby with the bath water here, holding on only to the Bible, while rejecting charismatic experiences. The trouble is, Luther claimed to vet his doctrine through the Scripture (*sola scriptura*), when, as we have seen, Scripture overwhelmingly advocates charismatic experience. The Bible also says not to *"think of men above that which is written* [in Scripture]*, that no one of you be puffed up for one against another"* (1 Cor. 4:6). *Both* Luther and Müntzer went "above that which was written in Scripture" in this case.

19. See Exod. 20:18-22; Heb. 12:18-25.

Chapter 11
A Review of the Rest of the Bible's Themes' Relation to the Baptism of the Holy Spirit

1. See Exod. 20; Heb. 12:18ff.

2. This is reminiscent of Rom. 11:29: "The *charismata* and the *calling* of God are not withdrawn." Does Paul intend *charismata* and *calling* to be synonymous, to describe the same thing?

3. See Isa. 6:1-7; Jer. 1:4-8; and Ezek. 1:3-28.

4. See Isa. 6:5-7; Jer. 1:6-19; Ezek. 1:28–3:4.

5. See Isa. 6:5,8; Jer. 1:6; Ezek. 1:28; 2:4,11.

6. See Isa. 6:5,9-12; Jer. 1:6-10;17-19; Ezek. 2:3–3:15;22-26.

7. See Isa. 6:9-12; Jer. 1:10-17; Ezek. 2:3-7; 3:4-21;24-27.

8. See Isa. 6:8; Jer. 1:2,4,9-13; Ezek. 2:8–3:4;10;11;14;24-26, esp. 27.

9. Based on a section from Ruthven, *What's Wrong with Protestant Theology*, 121–22.

10. The following is a true story. It used to be that every year in Springfield, Missouri, there would be a basketball game between a Pentecostal Bible college and a larger, cessationist Baptist Bible college. Every year for a long time the Pentecostals won. Finally, to rally the troops, the Baptists unfurled a huge banner taunting the Pentecostals that said, "We've got the Spirit!" The Pentecostals were ready for them. They taunted back with a banner of their own: "Once lost, always lost!" The point: Contrary to what both banners indicated, past spiritual experiences (good or bad) do not determine your present or future.

11. Jon Ruthven, "The 'Imitation of Christ' in Christian Tradition: Its Missing Charismatic Emphasis." *Journal of Pentecostal Theology* 16, no. 1 (Spring 2000): 60–77, accessed August 18, 2016, http://hopefaithprayer.com/books/The-Imitation-Christ -In-Christian-Tradition-Ruthven.pdf.

12. Christ is [secondarily] an example and pattern which we are to follow" (372). See "On Christ Crucified" in *Luthers Werke*, vol. 12 (Weimar: H. Böhlau, 1840).

13. See Matt. 10:1-39; Mark 6:7-12; Luke 9:1-6; 10:1-20.

14. See Mark 3:29; Luke 12:10.

15. See Acts 2:38-39, citing Isa. 59:21; cf. 2 Cor. 3; Heb. 8-12.

16. See Matt. 10; Mark 3:14-15; 6:7-13; Luke 9; 10; Acts 1:8.

17. See Heb. 8:6; 9:15; 12:24.

18. See Matt. 3:11; Mark 1:8; Luke 3:16; John 1:33; Acts 1:5; 2:38; 11:16.

19. See Isa. 59:21, cited in Acts 2:39 and Jer. 31:33, developed in 2 Cor. 3 and Heb. 8–12.

20. See Ezek. 36:26,27; 37:14; 39:29.

21. See Isa. 11:2; 42:1; 61:1-2; John 1:33; 14:26; 16:13; Acts 10:38 as well as Isa. 59:21; Acts 2:33; 9:17.

22. See Matt. 3:11; Mark 1:8; Luke 3:16; John 1:33; Acts 1:5; 2:38-39; 11:16.

23. See Rom. 15:18-19; 2 Cor. 12:12.

24. See Rom. 15:18-19; 2 Cor. 12:12; 1 Thess. 1:5, cf Acts 10:38.

Chapter 12
Holiness, Social Justice, Legalism, and Baptism in the Holy Spirit

1. To understand more about what I am saying in this paragraph, one should study Walter Wink's trilogy on The Powers. I agree with his insights on structural evil but believe he doesn't have enough emphasis on the personal dimension of evil and the reality of demons in the lives of people. See, for instance, Wink, *The Powers That Be: Theology for a New Millennium* (New York: Galilee Doubleday, 1998), 13–62.

Chapter 13
Revival and Holy Spirit Baptism

1. Bosworth, *Christ the Healer*, 189.

2. Wesley quoted in Jerry Steingard, "Preparing for Revival Fire," *Renewal Journal*, May 19, 2011, accessed November 1, 2016, https://renewaljournal.wordpress.com/2011/05/19/preparing-for-revival-by-jerry-steingard/.

3. See page 135 where Jon talks of these things.

4. J. Edwin Orr, "The First Great Awakening," *J. Edwin Orr*, accessed September 20, 2016, http://www.jedwinorr.com/resources/audio/COW_01.MP3.

5. Orr, "The Second Great Awakening," *J. Edwin Orr*, accessed September 20, 2016, http://www.jedwinorr.com/resources/audio/COW_02.MP3.

6. Ibid. Also contains remarks about this revival including "barking on the frontier." The Baptists didn't bark, but the Presbyterians did. However, Barton Stone, who was present, said, "There was no barking."

7. Elmer Towns, *The Ten Greatest Revivals Ever* (Ann Arbor, MI: Servant, 2000), 2-3.

8. Orr, "1858 Revival," *J. Edwin Orr*, accessed September 20, 2016, http://www.jedwinorr.com/resources/audio/COW_04. MP3. I have heavily drawn from Orr in these references because F. F. Bruce stated this about Orr: "Some men read history, some write it, and others make it. So far as the history of religious revivals is concerned, J. Edwin Orr belongs to all three categories." Moreover, Billy Graham said the following about Orr: "Dr. J. Edwin Orr, in my opinion, is one of the greatest authorities on the history of religious revivals in the Protestant world. I think that God has given him one of the greatest and most unique ministries anywhere in the nation...I know of no man who has a greater passion for worldwide revival or a greater love for the souls of men." I recommend the webpage dedicated to his teachings to any who are interested in learning more about revivals.

9. For more information read Synan's *The Holiness-Pentecostal Movement in the United States*.

10. Ibid.

11. Pew Research Center, "Global Christianity: A Report on the Size and Distribution of the World's Christian Population, December 9, 2011, accessed October 28, 2016, http://www .pewforum.org/2011/12/19/global-christianity-exec/.

12. The last time I spoke with John Wimber before he died, I told him about the position presented as the Vineyard position in Rich Nathan and Ken Wilson's book *Empowered Evangelicals,* which suggests Vineyard theology is identical to Evangelical theology in regard to the baptism in the Holy Spirit. I shared with him that I did not think he agreed with that position because he allowed for more diversity. John told me that he agreed that he allowed for more diversity. I encouraged him to make this known to the Vineyard, but I don't think he ever did so.

13. Randy Clark, *There Is More! The Secret to Experiencing God's Power to Change Your Life* (Bloomington, MN: Chosen Books, 2013).

14. Clark, *Lighting Fires* (Mechanicsburg, PA: Apostolic Network of Global Awakening, 2011).

Chapter 14
My Personal Testimonies and Others' Testimonies of Holy Spirit Baptism

1. For more on Rex and Lois Burgher and their Kingdom Life Ministry, visit https://klifemin.org/. Rex traveled with me longer than anyone, except Paul Martini. He and his wife Lois are ministers with integrity, and carry a powerful anointing for healing, impartation, and inner healing and deliverance training.

2. For Ben Scofield's biography visit https://globalawakening.com/ home/speakers/will-hart/28-speakers/181-ben-scofield. Ben was the first person God spoke to me clearly about having him travel with me as an intern.

3. View the whole interview, unedited, at https://www.youtube .com/watch?v=3dlFvOTdDqA&feature=youtu.be.

4. Because of this call and this baptism of the Spirit, Randy McMillan would spend the rest of his adult life in Colombia, where he would be instrumental in leading the prayer crusades that filled the stadium of Cali, where scores of thousands of Christians gathered to pray.

5. This account also appears in my book *The Healing Breakthrough* (Minneapolis, MN: Chosen, 2016), 71.

Conclusion

1. See Jon Ruthven's section, page 135. See Matt. 28:20, cf. John 14:18,28; 2 Cor. 3:17).
2. See Jon Ruthven's section, page 160.
3. Luke 11:13.
4. See Jon Ruthven's section, page 145.

Prayers

1. It is not normal for a person to receive all of these various manifestations. Usually it is one or a few, but rarely does one receive all of them at once.

BIBLIOGRAPHY

Ambrose. *On the Mysteries*. Translated by H. de Romestin, E. de Romestin, and H. T. F. Duckworth. *New Advent*. Accessed November 8, 2016. http://www.newadvent.org/fathers/3405.htm.

Aquinas, Thomas. *The Summa Theologiae of St. Thomas Aquinas*. 2nd ed. Translated by the Fathers of the English Dominican Province. *New Advent*. Accessed November 8, 2016. http://www.newadvent.org/summa/4072.htm.

Assemblies of God. *Our 16 Fundamental Truths*. March 1, 2010. Accessed December 28, 2016. http://www.ag.org/top/beliefs/statement_of_fundamental_truths/sft_full.cfm.

Augustine. *Sermon XXI: The Blasphemy Against the Holy Ghost*. Translated by R. G. MacMullen. *New Advent*. Accessed November 8, 2016. http://www.newadvent.org/fathers/160321.htm.

Baker, Heidi. "Pentecostal Experience: Towards a Reconstructive Theology of Glossolalia." Ph.D. dissertation, King's College London, 1996.

Barabas, Steven Barabas. *So Great Salvation: The History and Message of the Kewsick Convention*. Eugene, OR: Wipf & Stock, 1952.

Barrett, David B., ed. "Pentecostalism." *World Christian Encyclopedia: A Comparative Survey of Churches and Religions in the Modern World, A.D. 1900–2000.* 1st ed. Oxford, UK: Oxford University Press, 1982.

Basham, Don. *A Handbook on Holy Spirit Baptism.* Monroeville, PA: Whitaker Books, 1969.

Bittlinger, Arnold. *Gifts and Graces—A Commentary on 1 Corinthians 12-14.* Grand Rapids, MI: William B. Eerdmans Publishing Company, 1967.

Bosworth, F. F. *Christ the Healer.* Grand Rapids, MI: Chosen Books, 2000.

Brown, Colin, ed. *The New International Dictionary of New Testament Theology.* Grand Rapids, MI: Zondervan, 1986.

Bruner, Frederick Dale. *A Theology of the Holy Spirit.* Grand Rapids, MI: William B. Eerdmans, 1970.

Burgess, Stanley, ed. *Christian Peoples of the Spirit: A Documentary History of Pentecostal Spirituality from the Early Church to the Present.* New York: New York University Press, 2011.

Calvin, John. "Prefatory Address." *Institutes of the Christian Religion.*

Campolo, Tony. *Stories That Feed Your Soul.* Grand Rapids, MI: Baker, 2014.

Cantalamessa, Raniero. "Concerning the Baptism in the Holy Spirit." *Catholic Charismatic Renewal of New Orleans.* Accessed November 8, 2016. https://www.ccrno.org/WhatisBaptism.php.

_____. Sober Intoxication of the Spirit: Filled with the Fullness of God. Cincinnati, OH: Servant Books, 2005.

_____. "Charismatic Movement—Vatican Promotion." *YouTube.* Accessed October 28, 2016. https://www.youtube.com/ watch?v=J-QDOcDGDWA.

Choy, Leona Frances. Powerlines: What Great Evangelicals Believed About the Holy Spirit, 1850–1930. Christian Publications, 1990.

Chrysostom, John. *Commentary on Hebrews* 6: 1-2.

Clark, Glenn. "Jennie Evans Moore Seymour—Vanguard of Pentecost." *Charisma Magazine*. November 30, 2003. http://www.charismamag.com/site-archives/24-uncategorised/9826-jennie-evans-moore-seymour-vanguard-of-pentecost.

Clark, Randy. *Changed in a Moment.* Mechanicsburg, PA: Global Awakening, 2010.

———. *The Healing Breakthrough.* Minneapolis, MN: Chosen, 2016.

———. *There Is More! The Secret to Experiencing God's Power to Change Your Life.* Bloomington, MN: Chosen Books, 2013.

Cohen, Harold. "Baptized in the Holy Spirit." *Catholic Charismatic Renewal of New Orleans.* Accessed November 8, 2016. https://www.ccrno.org/WhatisBaptism.php.

Congar, Yves. *I Believe in the Holy Spirit.* Translated by David Smith. New York: Crossroad, 2005.

Cox, Leo G. *John Wesley's Concept of Sin.* Accessed December 28, 2016. https://biblicalstudies.org.uk/pdf/bets/vol05/5-1_cox.pdf.

Crawford, Mary. *The Shantaung Revival.* Mechanicsburg, PA: Apostolic Network of Global Awakening, 2005.

Culpepper, Robert H. *Evaluating the Charismatic Movement: A Theological and Biblical Appraisal.* Valley Forge, PA: Judson Press, 1977.

Cyprian. *Epistle 72.12 to Jubaianus, Concerning the Baptism of Heretics.* Translated by Robert Ernest Wallis. *New Advent.* Accessed November 8, 2016. http://www.newadvent.org/fathers/050672.htm.

———. *Epistle 74 to Cornelius.* Translated by Robert Ernest Wallis. *New Advent.* Accessed November 8, 2016. http://www.newadvent.org/fathers/050674.htm.

Cyril. *Lectures.* Translated by Edwin Hamilton Gifford. *New Advent.* Accessed November 8, 2016. http://www.newadvent.org/fathers/310103.htm.

_____. "Documents of the Second Ecumenical Council A.D. 381." Translated by Henry R. Percival. *Orthodoxia.org.* Accessed November 8, 2016. http://www.orthodoxa.org/GB/orthodoxy/canonlaw/canons2econcileGB.htm.

Drummond, Lewis, ed. *What the Bible Says: A Systematic Guide to Biblical Doctrines.* Nashville, TN: Abingdon Press, 1975.

Dunn, James. *Baptism in the Holy Spirit: A Re-examination of the New Testament Teaching on the Gift of the Spirit in Relation to Pentacostalism Today.* Philadelphia, PA: The Westminster Press, 1970.

_____. "Rediscovering the Spirit." *Expository Times* 84, no. 1 (October 1972).

_____. "Spirit and Kingdom." *Expository Times* 80, no. 2 (1970).

_____. "Spirit in the New Testament." *New International Dictionary of New Testament Theology.* Grand Rapids, MI: Zondervan, 1999.

Ervin, Howard M. *Conversion-Initiation and the Baptism in the Holy Spirit.* Peabody, MA: Hendrickson Publishers, 1984.

Emesenus, Eusebius Emesenus. "Sermon on Pentecost" in *Corpus Christianorum, Series Latina.* CCSL 101:338.

Eusebius. *Church History.* Translated by Arthur Cushman McGiffert. *New Advent.* Accessed November 8, 2016. http://www.newadvent.org/fathers/250106.htm.

Fee, Gordon D. *Gospel and Spirit: Issues in New Testament Hermaneutics.* Peabody, MA: Hendrickson Publishers, Inc., 1991.

_____. *God's Empowering Presence—The Holy Spirit in the Letters of Paul.* Peabody, MA: Hendrickson Publishers, Inc, 1994.

_____. *Paul, the Spirit, and the People of God.* Peabody, MA: Hendrickson Publishers, 1996.

Finney, Charles. *Charles G. Finney: An Autobiography.* Old Tappan, NJ: Fleming H. Revell Company, 1876.

_____. *Memoirs of Rev. Charles G. Finney.* New York, NY: A. S. Barnes & Company, 1876.

_____. *Revivals of Religion*. The Christian Classics, 700 Club Edition. Virginia Beach, VA: CBN University Press, 1978.

Fournier, Keith A. "A Current of Grace: Address of Pope Francis to the Charismatic Renewal Conference in Rome." *Catholic Online*. Accessed October 28, 2016. http://www.catholic.org/news/international/europe/story.php?id=55674.

Graham, Billy. *The Holy Spirit: Activating God's Power in Your Life*. Waco, TX: Word Books Publisher, 1978.

Gordon, A. J. *The Ministry of the Spirit*. Philadelphia, PA: Judson Press, 1984.

Greear, J.D. "The Most Important Thing About the Holy Spirit." Interview by Jen Pollock Michel. *Christianity Today*. January 5, 2015.

Green, Michael. *Evangelism in the Early Church*. Grand Rapids, MI: Eerdmans, 2003.

Green, Richard. *John Wesley—Evangelist*. *Wesley Center Online*. Accessed November 1, 2016. http://wesley.nnu.edu/john-wesley/john-wesley-evangelist/john-wesley-evangelist-chapter-6/.

Grudem, Wayne. *Systematic Theology—An Introduction to Biblical Doctrine*. Grand Rapids, MI: Zondervan, 1994.

Hanson, Don. *Knowing the Holy Ghost*. 2nd ed. 2007. *Lulu.com*. Accessed October 31, 2016.

Hart, Larry. "A Critique of American Pentecostal Theology." Ph.D. dissertation. The Southern Baptist Theological Seminary, 1976.

Herber, Reginald. *The Whole Works of the Right Rev. Jeremy Taylor, D.D., Lord Bishop of Down, Connor, and Dromore: With a Life of the Author, and a Critical Examination of His Writings*. Vol. 5. Oxford, England, 1828.

_____. *Holy Father's Speech for the World Congress of Ecclesial Movements and New Communities*. Accessed December 28, 2016. http://www .vatican.va/roman_curia/pontifical_councils/laity/documents/rc_pc_laity_doc_27051998_movements-speech-hf_en.html.

International Catholic Charismatic Renewal Services (ICCRS). *Baptism in the Holy Spirit.* Vatican City, Italy: Doctrinal Commission of ICCRS, 2012.

Jerome. *The Dialogue Against the Luciferians.* Translated by W. H. Fremantle, G. Lewis, and W. G. Martley. *New Advent.* Accessed November 8, 2016. http://www.newadvent.org/fathers/3005.htm.

Jones, Tom. "Divine Encounters: Analysis of Encounters that Shape Lives." D.Min. dissertation, United Theological Seminary, 2013.

Keener, Craig. *Miracles: The Credibility of the New Testament Accounts.* Grand Rapids, MI: Baker Academic, 2011.

Kendall, R.T. *Understanding Theology—The Means of Developing a Healthy Church in the 21st Century.* Ross-shire, UK: Geanies House, Reprint, 1998.

Kidd, Thomas. *George Whitefield: America's Spiritual Founding Father.* Princeton, NJ: Yale University Press, 2014.

_____. "More Doctrine Than a Person': Evangelicals and the Holy Spirit." *The Anxious Bench.* December 2, 2014. Accessed August 8, 2016. http://www.patheos.com/blogs/anxiousbench/2014/12/more-a-doctrine-than-a-person-evangelicals-and-the-holy-spirit/.

Lawler, Ronald, Donald Wuerl, and Thomas Comerford Lawler, eds., *The Teaching of Christ: A Catholic Catechism for Adults.* 2nd ed. Huntington, IN: Our Sunday Visitor, Inc., 2004.

Lawson, James Gilchrist. *Deeper Experiences of Famous Christians.* Anderson, IN: Warner Press, 1911.

Lederle, Henry I. *Theology with Spirit: The Future of the Pentecostal & Charismatic Movements in the 21st Century.* Word & Spirit Press, 2010. E-book.

Leo the Great. Letter to Nicetas. *Epistle LXXXIX.*

Lloyd-Jones, D. Martyn. *The Baptism and Gifts of the Spirit.* Edited by Christopher Catherwood. Grand Rapids, MI: Baker Books, 1984.

Logan, Alastair H. B. "Marcellus of Ancyra and Anti-Arian Polemic." *Studia Patristica*. Edited by Elizabeth A. Livingstone. Leuven, Belgium: Peeters Press, 1989.

Lumpkin. W. L. *Baptist Confessions of Faith*. Reprint Valley Forge, PA: Judson Press, 1974.

McDonnell, Killian, and Arnold Bittlinger. *The Baptism in the Holy Spirit as an Ecumenical Problem*. Notre Dame, IN: Charismatic Renewal Services, 1972.

McDonnell, Killian, and George T. Montague, eds. *Fanning the Flame: What Does Baptism in the Holy Spirit Have to Do with Christian Initiation?* Collegeville, MN: Liturgical Press, 1991.

Macchia, Frank D. *Baptized in the Spirit: A Global Pentecostal Theology*. Grand Rapids, MI: Zondervan, 2006.

MacNutt, Francis. "Being Baptized in the Holy Spirit." *Tentmaker*. May/June 2003. Accessed August 7, 2016. http://www.tentmaker.org/holy-spirit/baptized.htm.

_____. "My Search for the Spirit." *Christian Healing Ministries*. Spring 2014. Accessed August 18, 2016. https://www.christianhealingmin.org/index.php?option =com_content&view=article&id=626:my-search-for-the -spirit&catid=209&Itemid=458.

Mahan, Asa. *Baptism of the Holy Spirit*. Clifton, NY: Williams Publishers, 1880.

Menzies, William W. *Anointed to Serve: The Story of the Assemblies of God*. Springfield, MO: Gospel Publishing House, 1980.

Moore, Peter. "God Told Me To, Say 38% of Americans." *YouGov*. October 25, 2013. Accessed August 18, 2016. https://today.yougov.com/news/2013/10/25/god-told-me/.

Nathan, Rich, and Ken Wilson. *Empowered Evangelicals: Bringing Together the Best of the Evangelical and Charismatic Worlds*. Ann Arbor, MI: Servant Publications, 1995.

"On Christ Crucified." *Luthers Werke*. Vol. 12. Weimar: H. Böhlau, 1840.

Origen. "Homilies 1–14 on Ezekiel." *Ancient Christian Writers.* Washington, DC: Catholic University Press, 2001.

Orr, J. Edwin. "The First Great Awakening." *J. Edwin Orr.* Accessed September 20, 2016. http://www.jedwinorr.com/resources/audio/COW_01.Mp3.

———. "The Second Great Awakening." *J. Edwin Orr.* Accessed September 20, 2016. http://www.jedwinorr.com/resources/audio/COW_02.MP3.

———. "1858 Revival." *J. Edwin Orr.* Accessed September 20, 2016. http://www.jedwinorr.com/resources/audio/COW_04 .MP3.

O'Shea, William J. *Sacraments of Initiation.* Englewood Cliffs, NJ: Prentice-Hall, 1965.

Pavao, Paul. "Holy Spirit Baptism Quotes." *Christian History for Everyman.* Last modified 2014. Accessed August 18, 2016. http://www.christian-history.org/holy-spirit-baptism-quotes.html.

Pew Research Center. "Global Christianity: A Report on the Size and Distribution of the World's Christian Population." December 9, 2011. Accessed October 28, 2016. http://www .pewforum .org/2011/12/19/global-christianity-exec/.

Phillips, Ron. *An Essential Guide to the Baptism in the Holy Spirit.* Lake Mary, FL: Charisma House, 2011.

Pierson, A. T. *The Keswick Movement: In Precept and Practice.* New York: Funk and Wagnall's, 1903.

Piper, John. "You Will Be Baptized with the Holy Spirit." Sermon, September 23, 1990. Accessed August 18, 2016. www.desiringgod.org/sermons/you-will-be-baptized-with-the-holy-spirit.

Plass, E. *What Luther Says.* St. Louis, MO: Concordia, 1959.

———. *Popes and the Charismatic Renewal.* Accessed December 28, 2016. http://www.lovecrucified.com/holy_spirit/charismatic_renewal/renewal_message_popes.html.

Ruthven, Jon. "Appendix on the Essentially Charismatic Nature of the Spirit's Activity." Ph.D. dissertation, Marquette University, 1989.

_____. "The 'Imitation of Christ' in Christian Tradition: Its Missing Charismatic Emphasis." *Journal of Pentecostal Theology* 16, no. 1 (Spring 2000): 60–77. Accessed August 18, 2016. http://hopefaithprayer.com/books/The-Imitation-Christ-In -Christian-Tradition-Ruthven.pdf.

_____. *On the Cessation of the Charismata: The Protestant Polemic on Postbiblical Miracles.* Tulsa, OK: Word & Spirit Press, 2011.

_____. *What's Wrong with Protestant Theology? Tradition vs. Biblical Emphasis.* Tulsa, OK: Word & Spirit Press, 2013.

Smith, Brittany. "More Than 1 in 4 Christians Are Pentecostal, Charismatic." *Christian Post Reporter.* December 21, 2011. Accessed October 31, 2016. http://www.christianpost.com/news/ more-than-1-in-4-christians-are-pentecostal-charismatic-65358/.

Smith, Harold B., ed. *Pentecostals from the Inside Out.* London, UK: Victor Books, 1990.

Steingard, Jerry. "Preparing for Revival Fire." *Renewal Journal.* May 19, 2011. Accessed November 1, 2016. https://renewaljournal.wordpress.com/2011/05/19/ preparing-for-revival-by-jerry-steingard/.

Stott, John R. W. *Baptism & Fullness—The Work of the Holy Spirit Today.* Downers Grove, IL: Intervarsity Press 1975.

Stronstad, Roger. *The Charismatic Theology of St. Luke.* Peabody, MA: Hendrickson Publishers, 1984.

Suenens, Léon-Joseph. *A New Pentecost?* Translated by Francis Martin. New York: Seabury Press, Inc., 1975.

Synan, Vinson. *The Holiness-Pentecostal Movement in the United States.* Grand Rapids, MI: William B. Eerdmans, 1971.

Taylor, Jack R. *The Hallelujah Factor.* Nashville, TN: Broadman Press, 1983.

Taylor, Jeremy. Introduction to *Discourse of Confirmation.* Ann Arbor, MI: Text Creation Partnership, 2012.

Telford, John. *The Life of John Wesley.* London, UK: The Epworth Press.

Tertullian. "Homily on Baptism." Edited and translated by Ernest Evans. *Tertullian.org.* 1964. Accessed October 31, 2016. www .tertullian.org/articles/evans_bapt/evans_bapt_index.htm.

———. *Tertullian's Treatises: Concerning Prayer, Concerning Baptism.* Translated by Alexander Soutner. New York: Macmillan Company, 1919.

Torrey, R. A. *The Baptism with the Holy Spirit.* Minneapolis, MN: Bethany Fellowship, 1972.

———. *The Holy Spirit: Who He Is and What He Does.* Alachua, FL: Bridge-Logos, 2008.

Towns, Elmer. *The Ten Greatest Revivals Ever.* Ann Arbor, MI: Servant, 2000.

Tozer, A. W. *How to Be Filled with the Holy Spirit.* Camp Hill, PA: Christian Publications, n.d.

Tyson, Tommy. "Biography." *Tommy Tyson.* Accessed August 18, 2016. http://www.tommytyson.org/index.php?option=com _content&view=article&id=51&Itemid=55.

Vermes, Geza. *Jesus the Jew: A Historian's Reading of the Gospels.* Philadelphia, PA: Fortress Press, 1973.

Weakley Jr., Clare George. *The Nature of Revival: John Wesley, Charles Wesley and George Whitefield.* Minneapolis, MN: Bethany House, 1987.

Welchel, Tommy, and Michelle P. Griffith. *True Stories of the Miracles of Azusa Street and Beyond.* Shippensburg, PA: Destiny Image, 2013.

Wimber, John. *Power Healing.* San Francisco, CA: HarperCollins, 1987.

Wiley, H. Orton, *Christian Theology. Wesley Center Online.* Accessed November 11, 2016. http://wesley .nnu.edu/noncanonical-literature/henry-orton-wiley/ h-orton-wiley-christian-theology-chapter-29/.

Williams, J. Rodman. *Renewal Theology: Salvation, the Holy Spirit, and Christian Living.* Vol. 2. Grand Rapids, MI: Zondervan, 1990.

Wink, Walter. *The Powers That Be: Theology for a New Millennium.* New York: Galilee Doubleday, 1998.

Wood, George O. "From the General Superintendent." *Assemblies of God.* Accessed August 18, 2016. http://agchurches.org/Sitefiles/Default/RSS/AG.org%20TOP/WoodRevivalStatement.pdf.

Wood, Lawrence W. *The Meaning of Pentecost in Early Methodism.* Lanham, MD: Scarecrow Press, 2002.

_____. *The Work Claiming to Be the Constitutions of the Holy Apostles.* Translated by Irah Chase. New York: D. Appleton, 1848.

About Randy Clark

Randy Clark, with a D.Min. from United Theological Seminary, is the founder of Global Awakening, a teaching, healing, and impartation ministry that crosses denominational lines. An in-demand international speaker, he leads the Apostolic Network of Global Awakening and travels extensively for conferences, international missions, leadership training, and humanitarian aid. Randy and his wife, DeAnne, live in Pennsylvania.